To Joan,

"What a girl!"

Love,

Bob

The Other Side of Success

... And All Its Empty Promises

Robert E. Draper

iUniverse, Inc.
New York   Bloomington

The Other Side of Success
... And All Its Empty Promises

The views expressed in this work are solely those of the author and do not necessarily reflect the views of the publisher, and the publisher hereby disclaims any responsibility for them.

iUniverse books may be ordered through booksellers or by contacting:

iUniverse
1663 Liberty Drive
Bloomington, IN 47403
www.iuniverse.com
1-800-Authors (1-800-288-4677)

Because of the dynamic nature of the Internet, any Web addresses or links contained in this book may have changed since publication and may no longer be valid.

ISBN: 978-0-595-52735-9 (pbk)
ISBN: 978-0-595-51571-4 (cloth)
ISBN: 978-0-595-62786-8 (ebk)

Printed in the United States of America

iUniverse rev. date: 3/20/2009

Ah, love, let us be true
To one another! for the world, which seems
To lie before us like a land of dreams,
So various, so beautiful, so new,
Hath really neither joy, nor love, nor light,
Nor certitude, nor peace, nor help for pain;
And we are here as on a darkling plain
Swept with confused alarms of struggle and flight,
Where ignorant armies clash by night.

—Matthew Arnold, "Dover Beach"

Contents

Preface

A while back, a friend named David asked my opinions about business, success, and life. Because I care for him, I have answered in detail by writing this book.

At the outset, though, I will give him and the rest of you reading it a forewarning: most likely, the opinions you find here will not be what you would expect.

Let me explain. When I was a little younger than David was at the time this book was published, I was well on the way to what many considered a life of achievement. A beneficiary of early business success, I was a CEO by thirty-five, sure that I had "the goods" needed for accomplishment and that only better things would come my way. And, from a business viewpoint, they did: the company I headed growing more successful each year.

What I found surprising about that, even shocking, was that the greater the success, the less gratifying it seemed. Don't misunderstand me. I'm not going to suggest in this book that there is something wrong with advancement or that you should in any way cease to do your best to aspire to become more successful, whatever your career path. I will, however, urge you not to let what is commonly accepted as success fool you. In and of itself, what is so loosely termed "success" is no more than a pretty box tied with a fancy ribbon, holding nothing inside. Part of the burden of this book will be to convince you of that and to describe in detail what real success is.

Introduction: My Story

Throughout much of my dogma-infused early life, independent thinking was so frowned upon it may as well have been labeled the eighth deadly sin.

My uneducated parents were far from stupid, but they were also far from adventuresome in their thinking. They were decent, poor, strict, hardworking, and highly religious Irish immigrants to New York. My mother came to this country because she had neither parents nor opportunity on the small farm on which her grandparents raised her. My father, one of nine fatherless children, left Dublin for essentially the same reasons.

In New York, my parents met, married, and had three children: me, my sister, and then my brother. When I was four, my family moved from our apartment in Yonkers to a ten-room (unheated) farmhouse on the outskirts of the Lincolndale reform school, near Poughkeepsie, where my father was employed as a chauffeur and a handyman.

There I learned, among other things, that bulls can be ferocious, stoves can burn, and getting stitches can hurt. I learned that chickens do run around for a while after their heads are chopped off, that dogs sometimes run away and don't come back, and that accepting a baby rabbit you covet from a Christian brother who stole it from a reform-school boy produces guilt rather than pleasure. I also learned that some teachers hit first graders for not paying attention and that woodchucks caught in traps in vegetable gardens squeal loudly and die slowly when beaten to death with crowbars.

When I was six, my family moved back to New York. Our new home was a one-bedroom, first-floor apartment in a five-story, fifty-family tenement on a block filled with similar buildings in the Kingsbridge section of the Bronx. My father was the custodian of the large Catholic church down the block and the Catholic school around the corner. In the Bronx, my opportunities to learn multiplied; my brain had to make adjustments at every turn.

First, I had to learn to adjust to the inner crowdedness. I went from having my own big bedroom to sharing a tiny one with four others, from eating in a large country kitchen to one no bigger than a large closet, and from living in a free-standing house to an apartment completed by a small living room, a tiny bathroom, and regular visits from cockroaches and an occasional mouse or two.

Then there was the noise. The apartments were built around an open courtyard, and in good weather the clamor pouring in from the streets and out from the other apartments was overwhelming. The family across the courtyard from us featured a drunken, widowed father with three daughters, their drunken boyfriends, and parties every weekend. Three flights up was a friend's mother, an alcoholic married to an alcoholic, who would stick her head out the window at 2:00 a.m. and scream, "He's choking me! He's killing me!" On the floor below them lived the mother of four daughters, who had "breakdowns" and was often "sent away." On the other side lived another drunken father who was sporadically challenged to come out and fight by one drunk or another from down the street; one of those threats resulted in a knife fight on the stairs. Then there was the lady who dropped milk cartons filled with water out of her fourth-floor window to shut kids up, the thief on the fifth floor, and the enormous longshoreman who frequently came staggering home drunk at noon. (It was not uncommon to see a man staggering down the street in the daytime.) However, along with numerous other such characters, there were also many hardworking and sober families doing their best to survive in a tough, poverty-stricken world.

At first, it felt like I had landed in hell. Back in the country, on the farm, I had had no playmates other than my sister. Now I found myself thrust onto streets teeming with children of all ages, everyone virtually bouncing off of each other. This harsh environment had much to offer in toughening you up, but little room for niceties. I quickly learned that you either figured out how to cope, or were, like some of the more timid, doomed to hide away in trepidation in your apartment. The school, unimaginably, was even worse. It was large, crowded, and run like a prison, an institution of Catholic learning staffed mainly with sadistic nuns whose title "Mother" was a misnomer of the highest order.

I was not very big or strong at the time, and while well able to hold my own in the ballgames that city kids played, I was far from being a tough guy in a land overpopulated with them. So for a while, I competed mainly in the classroom. Yet it wasn't long before it dawned on me that being able to answer every question the teacher asked was not the road to the acceptance I sought. I therefore throttled back and choked down that talent. Punishment at school as well as regular strappings and the like at home kept my grades up but also nurtured my resentment of the bullying by my teachers and parents. At that point, I tried religious fervor, volunteering as an altar boy for a while, but the haughty attitude and drunkenness of some of the priests, together with the ignorant outlook and general meanness of the nuns and the mumbo jumbo of their non-answers to my tough questions, increasingly grated on me.

I can remember in the sixth grade, for example, being taught about God's omniscience and our free will. I had said to the nun, "Let me understand this. God knows all things, past, present, and to come?"

"Yes," she replied.

"And he gives us the gift of free will?" I asked.

"Yes," she said again.

"And," I continued, "we can then misuse that free will in such a way that we can end up in hell forever?"

"Yes."

"But if God knows all things in the present and to come, then he must know before he gives us free will that we will misuse it and end up in hell. So how could that be?"

To which I received the usual reply to questions of that sort: "It's a mystery."

All in all, I was already well mystified and quite dissatisfied. I was bright, but there was no payoff for it. My parents wanted more, my schoolmates wanted less, and neither answer reduced the imbalance of the personal conflict I was experiencing. The living conditions hardly ameliorated it either, nor did the pitiful wages paid to my father, which kept us there. From banging on the radiators, along with the rest of the building's tenants, for heat in the mornings, to wearing used clothing from church drives, to eating poor-quality food and just dealing with the general lack of money, everything left me frustrated.

Bullying weaker children left me feeling guilty, and being pushed around by older or tougher ones made me resentful. My father's constant presence in the school was far from a blessing, and his position as head usher at the church, along with my mother's wishes for my perfection, seemed to leave them with the expectation that I should be well above average in brightness and industriousness. With some exceptions, I was, at least through the first year of high school, where in exchange for mean nuns we received even meaner, face-slapping Christian brothers.

By the time I arrived at Cardinal Hayes, the huge, boring, uncaring factory of a high school I was sent to in my sophomore year, I was fed up with obedience and its paltry rewards. And when the overly aggressive brother in geometry class rudely refused to answer my question one day, something snapped. I thought, to put it politely, "Screw you!" At that exact moment, I packed up obedience and gave it a long rest.

Beginning the following day, I began to skip school regularly, at first for a day or two at a time, and soon after for three or four days. Since this was before we could afford a telephone, I got away with it. Unfortunately, though, I didn't get away with it for long. A report card with unexplained absences and failing grades landed in my hands, requiring my parents' signatures. Anticipating their response, I went into a panic. So I used my fertile fourteen-year-old brain and came up with a plan. First, I told the school I had lost the report card. Soon after, in possession of two, I used correction fluid on one, gave myself respectable grades, and offered it to my parents for signature. I then forged their signatures on the undoctored one and returned it to the school. The scheme worked perfectly. I was free again.

Free for what? Free to roam the streets of Manhattan, sneak into movies, shoplift costume jewelry at Macy's and trade it for time at the tables in darkened pool halls. Free to disobey, at long last, in every way. I had not reached tough, but I was well beyond smart, and firmly on the pathway into the dark valley of wild.

Finally, though, the semester ended and a real report card arrived in the mail, and with it, the day of reckoning. My parents were stunned. My father beat me to the point of accidentally rupturing my spleen, and I spent a month in the hospital. Only years later did I realize that the truly difficult roles in this situation were the ones being played by the man and his wife standing by the hospital bed, and not by the boy in it.

At the time, though, despite the beating, it seemed to me that I had gained an advantage. My father could no longer threaten me physically, being afraid after the accident to lay a hand on me, and in my youthful rebelliousness and selfishness, I didn't care much for his or anyone else's goodwill. So I used this advantage to feed my rebellion. Now, clearly, this rebelliousness was strictly my problem. Despite their strictness and my father's mistake, my parents were not bad people, and having been raised in the same environment, my siblings were cooperative: my sister ending up with a master's degree from New York University and a fellowship to Wharton, and my brother a master's from Columbia. But my way, filled with self-imposed difficulties, took a far different course.

Over the following two years, I repeated a rebellious, self-destructive pattern, acting like an idiotic hoodlum, getting ejected from three additional high schools in fewer than eighteen months. I often thought myself akin to a prisoner of war, with a duty to escape when possible and a commitment to keep trying if recaptured. I ran away from home numerous times, sleeping in hallways, on rooftops, in subways, and the like. While still fourteen, I hitchhiked from New York City and got as far as Virginia. But then, waking up there early one morning and looking down a long roadway, I thought, "I'm too young for this," and turned back.

Soon after that, at age fifteen, along with another boy from the neighborhood, I made it as far as Daytona Beach, Florida, returning home after we were arrested for vagrancy, a trick used by the police to get us to leave. Later, still fifteen, I returned to Florida by myself, that time securing a job as a page boy at a hotel beach club in Palm Beach. School bored and annoyed me, but being paid for work seemed to do away with my rebellion.

Living in Florida was good for me; I learned how to take care of myself and even how, when it was required, to cooperate. Along the way, I read constantly and indiscriminately, educating myself on my own terms.

I remained in Palm Beach for about four months, sharing a room in the hotel's workers' dorms with a truly decent fellow who was justifiably proud of his heritage as a full-blooded American Indian. He worked as a lifeguard, and he both protected me and helped me to grow up.

At sixteen, I returned home and got a job as an accounting clerk at ACF Industries in Manhattan. And, for a while, I attended a joke called continuation school. Although I went to work without fail and always did a fine job, back in my old neighborhood I was as wild as ever, as were many of the hundreds of other teenagers in that area. It was still the Bronx, and even though my parents rarely drank, and moderately at that, much of the world around me was still drunk and violent. In Florida, I had worked and associated with older guys and, like any impressionable kid, loved it. At home, I began to do the same, hanging on the outskirts of a gang too old for me, in bars well before I was seventeen—still rebellious, just in a different way.

Then a number of us together made what we considered a smart move: we joined the army shortly before the veterans' benefits ran out. Unfortunately, to me and my friends, the army was just another big school. In my second week, a guy from the neighborhood who had been in for six weeks got me to hop the fence with him, and we headed back to the neighborhood to drink for the night. In my sixth week, when I was supposed to be on the firing range, another guy and I were caught in the Post Exchange drinking coffee. Toward the end of our basic training, five of us from the neighborhood were marched up and down in front of the company as examples of what soldiers should *not* be like. After three years in the army, while also starting college courses and reading classics, I left at the exact same level I had entered. This was no mean feat in a place of automatic promotions. I guess they felt pretty much the same about me as I did them, though; at the end, the captain in charge of re-enlistment, seeing it was me in front of his desk, replaced his usual enthusiastic pitch with a finger pointed toward the door.

Now fit and strong enough for my size, I returned home to the neighborhood with its dinginess, crowdedness, and general aggression, and with its wild and violent bars, of which there were about twenty within three blocks of my home. I found a new job and continued to work in Manhattan, attended Pace University at night on the GI Bill, and drank with scores of others on the weekends.

After a while, I went off to California for three months but couldn't find a foothold there. When I came back, I found a sales job with potential at Friden Business Machines. I then got married to get out of my parents' house and because everyone else I knew had, drank, fought in the bars, worked hard, succeeded at work, read, studied, succeeded some more. Then, as I began to earn a respectable income, I vaguely started to wonder what life was all about. After ending up with sixty-three stitches one night from being kicked about the head and face in one more bar fight—it *was* a rough neighborhood—I decided my choices were either to get a weapon or move beyond the familiar: in other words, relocate.

Having found a modicum of sanity by then in the career I was beginning to build in Manhattan, my wife and I moved to New Jersey, and I put bar fights behind me forever. But I continued to party heavily in my spare time while working hard and living the high life in Manhattan, rapidly reaching a level of business success well beyond my wildest boyhood dreams. Back then, everyone I knew drank to excess. Manhattan in the evening was an ongoing uproarious party. The people I worked with all drank. Also, in the suburban development in Matawan, New Jersey, where we now lived, everyone drank. And in the old neighborhood, which I visited regularly and where everyone I grew up with still lived, everyone I knew drank. If you had enough money, and by then I did, it was always party time.

After a while, I got fed up with partying and dedicated myself to being a father and building my career. In short order, I moved from sales to an assistant manager's position in business equipment.

Soon after that, I was offered a sales manager's job in California, which I accepted. I built a sales force there, partially out of guys who had worked for me in New York or had attended school with me. Shortly thereafter, I was made a branch manager.

Before I knew it, I was on to larger branches in different places, and then on to division management on the East Coast, all in a dizzying series of promotions and better jobs that paid more and more money. Then my former boss in California, now in the clinical laboratory business, called and offered me a vice president's position in his new company. My initial response was, "Thanks, but no thanks." But when he added, "You can make your headquarters in San Diego," I replied, "Let me call you back." I spoke to my wife, and within an hour I decided to accept his offer, not because I cared for the job, but because I was tired of the winter's cold and long commutes. In addition, having been to San Diego a few times, I knew we would enjoy living there. Within a year, my boss had moved on to buy his own company and I had his job, and not long after, a CEO's title and business success in every direction I looked.

After fourteen years of marriage, which included having five children within the first seven years, I got divorced to neither my wife's nor my own surprise. I then met a wonderful woman named Kathy, remarried, and moved into a house across the street from the ocean in beautiful La Jolla, California, not far from where my children lived. I continued to party, now in a more sophisticated fashion. I traveled the world on the Concorde and private jets, staying in suites at the Carlyle in Manhattan and others like it elsewhere. I dealt with my oldest daughter's life-threatening leukemia and my oldest son's decline into the depths of drug and alcohol abuse, which eventually killed him. I did my best to be a responsible divorced husband and parent, working, playing, succeeding even more, but above all, beginning to wonder why, with all my effort and success, I was not more than superficially satisfied and underneath that, in fact, miserable.

Sure, I had my share of problems, but many people had as many and some a lot more. And I had so much more to be grateful for than the average person: a beautiful and caring wife, a lovely home, power, money, position, country clubs, travel, nice cars, good relationships with my children, friends, and a great living environment. Yet somehow, all of that was nowhere near enough. These things offered me no real contentment or peace of mind, only distractions from my discontent.

So I tried new things. I started to help others, which seemed to help me. And, without any particular volition, I started to contemplate my life. I began to put drinking aside, sometimes for weeks and other times for months at a time. I studied and I wondered. I helped more people. I floated around in our swimming pool for an entire summer, doing little more than musing about my feelings, and then finally exiting the water late one Sunday afternoon thinking, "There simply has to be a different way to live than this."

This was particularly strange, at least for me. I had concluded long before that money would be the answer to all of life's problems, but now that I had it, I knew that it was not. Not knowing what else to do with this foreign way of thinking, I simply carried on as I had, drinking less, helping more, continuing to be more and more successful in business, but still pondering and reflecting, and thinking deeply. After doing this for some time and discovering no lasting answers, I became somewhat depressed and almost gave up hope.

Then one Friday afternoon, a friend of mine named Jim called, inviting me to join him and a doctor friend of ours, Paul, on a visit to a woman whom he said had psychic powers. I had great admiration for Jim, whom I was helping financially and, at times, physically. He had been an athletic young fellow, the manager of the health club to which I belonged and my occasional racquetball partner, until the previous year, when he turned instantly from the picture of health into a quadriplegic in a hang-gliding accident.

I respected Jim, who never let his stunning physical reversal keep him down emotionally. But despite my respect for him and for Paul, and despite Jim's respect for this so-called psychic woman, I declined. I had no interest in such nonsense. When he called again later in the day, I declined once more. For some reason, though, he called again over the weekend and then a fourth time on Monday morning. Finally, I said, "All right, Jim, if it is that important to you, I'll go along just to keep you and Paul company."

Later that morning, a sunny January day in 1982, we drove to a modest but pleasant home in central San Diego. When we arrived, who greeted us at the door? Not some dark-haired mysterious woman with an odd gleam in her eye, but a pleasant-faced chubby Mrs. Claus of a white-haired woman, with ruddy cheeks and a big grin. Paul introduced her to me as Adele. After serving us tea, soda, and cake at a sturdy wooden table, Adele cleared it off and got Jim's assent to speak to one of his deceased relatives (I know, I know, here is where it gets trippy). She then put her hand on the table and, as I looked on in astonishment, that end of the table jumped about a foot in the air.

I was stunned. This was not possible. This sweet little grandmotherly woman, with her sense of humor and ready smile, had just broken the law of gravity before my eyes. I immediately looked under the table for wires or springs or some kind of explanation, but there was nothing hidden and no way to explain what was happening. She then suggested that Jim ask the table a question. (Again, I know this sounds weird beyond belief. But if it seems that way to you when reading this, please try to understand how utterly strange and unreasonable it felt to me when watching it.)

Jim asked a question and the table tapped out an answer, the number of taps representing a letter in the alphabet. For example, it tapped two times for the letter *b* and five times for *e* to spell out the word *be*, tapping not quietly, but authoritatively. This went on for a while. As I observed, it blew my mind to think that I was sitting in this nice little kitchen, with the sun streaming through the window, next to this wonderful young man and this medical doctor, both of whom I knew to be normal and intelligent, watching a sweet elderly woman do something that seemed like magic, but which, while inexplicable, clearly was not.

At some point, she looked over at me and said, "You don't believe this, do you, Bob?" I mumbled a polite reply, to which she responded, "Let's try it with you."

I declined, but she and the others insisted. I declined and they insisted. Finally, I said okay, and that's how it began.

"Is there anyone you would like to talk to?" she asked me.

"Well, my father died some while ago," I said, going along to see what would happen.

"Fine, what was his name?" she asked. "We'll call him into the table."

At this point, I'm thinking, "Sure, you're about to call my father into this table. I suppose later, I'll lift up off this seat, levitate out the window, and fly up onto the roof. What the hell is going on here, and why are these other two guys so amused at my consternation?" But already into it, I went along.

She said, "Ask the table a question only your father would know."

"Okay," I said to the table, "tell me your middle name."

The table, speaking for my father, without hesitation spelled out "Francis." I was flabbergasted. No one in the room knew that fact but me.

Next, she had me ask a few more questions, which the table also got right. Then she said, "You still don't believe this, do you?"

Again I mumbled a polite response, after which she said, "All right, Bob, ask the table a question in silence."

"This should be good," I thought. Then, without uttering a word, I mentally said to this normal kitchen table with which I was having this absurd conversation, "Tell me the name of the section of Dublin in which you were raised."

Again without hesitation, the table spelled out "Fairview," which was the right answer. As it did so, something snapped in my mind, kind of like it had with the Christian brother in my first high school. But this time, however, it snapped in a positive sense.

And, at that particular moment, in that particular kitchen, under that strange circumstance—all because I accepted that if the law of gravity could be broken and tables could accurately answer silent questions, anything might be possible—my life changed forever. I thought, "If this is possible, anything is possible," and I found myself repeating this theme for the rest of the day. To Adele, Jim, and Paul, I remain grateful for that to this day.

I saw Adele a number of times after that and watched her comfort many grieving people over the loss of loved ones. I never did believe that the deceased communicated through her table, though. After a while, I came to my own understanding of what was happening in that little house where she never accepted money, refused a number of requests to go on *60 Minutes*, and always fed and gave copies of her book to everyone, including the movie and rock stars who came to see her. She was psychic and telekinetic. She could put a glass of water on the table, tilt the table up a foot and a half or more, and the glass would never move or the water slosh out. She could go to other places and, with far heavier tables, simply lay her hand on the table and have one end leap in the air and answer questions in the same manner. I eventually concluded that her psychic ability enabled her to read a person's mind, probably unconsciously, and so without any awareness she was doing so, she would be able to automatically stop the table at the appropriate letter to give any person the correct answer.

Yet for me, what mattered more than finding an explanation was that from the moment I left her house that first day, something had shifted deep within my mind. I had realized with the utmost certainty that there was much more to life than I had ever suspected, and it was this realization that gave me insight into how I would find the satisfaction I had been seeking: through learning. Learning about the many things out there that were open to me that I had not yet discovered. I was a man who had been in despair, at the edge of hopelessness, who now had great hope.

It was thus that I began to study ever more intensely, reading everything from history to psychology, philosophy, and metaphysics, and even a bit of quantum mechanics. I never drank again, I did my best to be helpful and not harmful to others, and, like any other human, I continued to make plenty of mistakes. But from that point on, I saw everything that happened in my life, whether good or bad, as positive, because I had become dedicated to learning from it all.

It was ironic: I was the recalcitrant student for whom learning was now the main purpose of life. And no matter how difficult things became, I remained essentially upbeat. I had finally found meaning in what I had been close to concluding was a meaningless world.

In the following pages, I will try to convey in an abbreviated form what I have learned over my many years of study, reflection, and experience. Then I will discuss how I have applied that learning to my life and to the way in which I define success, and how you can do the same. In Part I, I will outline many of the problems inherent in the business world today, demonstrate their true cause, and talk about how to overcome them. The second section expands on the ideas introduced in the first, revealing the common misconceptions that prevent you from experiencing real success. It also describes how lasting success is attainable through practicing a shift in attitude and focus. Finally, Part III extends the application of these ideas into your everyday life to demonstrate how to uncover, harness, and put into service your innate strength and move beyond what's known as success in order to truly become the leader—of yourself—you have always sought to be.

At times, I will quote directly from people like Epictetus, Plato, Krishnamurti, and Kenneth Wapnick; at others, I will simply relate common threads that run through the teachings of all the great thinkers without offering a specific attribution. It is my hope that you will find their wisdom of as much assistance as I did.

PART I

BUSINESS

1
The Bad

The Middlemen

What is business or commerce? How did it start? And then, maybe more important, what has it become? To begin with a simple example, imagine three strangers in a chance encounter at a crossroads long ago. After chatting for a while, they discover that one raises cattle, another grows vegetables, and the third makes boots. Finding each other companionable, they decide to meet again the following week to engage in trade. After a few mutually beneficial meetings, each brings along a friend. One has a flock of egg-producing chickens, another weaves cloth, and the third makes cabinets, tables, and beds. These newcomers also engage in trade, to the increasing satisfaction of the group.

Soon after, other friends with different goods and skills are introduced into the mix, and Saturday, the meeting day, becomes "Fair Day at the Crossroads." As this activity continues and grows, it becomes apparent that if the fair is not to turn into chaos, the assistance of others will be required: people to set up booths and tables and to clean up after each fair, a printer to prepare notices of special or future events, someone to adjudicate disputes, a sheriff to keep thieves away and control crowds, and so on.

As no single merchant wants the responsibility for such matters, it is agreed a merchant's association will be formed, a fee levied on each sale to pay for these now necessary additional people and services, and a manager employed to take care of all of it. At this moment the concept of a middleman has entered the equation.

As time goes on, the role of the middleman—or manager— expands. He takes it upon himself to offer, for a fee of course, new services to the association: promoting the fair to those at farther distances, acting as a go-between for merchants whose increasing trades make it burdensome for them to haul their goods to market each week, collecting monies due and deposits, taking on the role of a guarantor of delivery, vouching for the integrity of certain sellers, and the like.

After a while, the activity of the middleman expands even further. He begins to offer the services of salespeople and accountants, cartage, warrants and guarantees, consumer loans, product and liability insurance, legal services, debt collection, and so forth. At this point the producers of the goods and services need provide only samples of their wares and capabilities and, eventually, only representations of them. Although some of them decide to hire their own accounting and sales and service forces, all remain dependent on the middleman for much of what takes place in their business transactions.

The middleman, being industrious and capable, as well as a thinker and a planner, continues to invent new ideas. He arranges for financing when a producer is affected by weather or other problems. He offers to exchange some of the fees due him for percentages of ownership in the properties, enterprises, and future production. He offers those who wish to remain at home the ability to do so, managing their booths, sales, and financial transactions for them. He forms a cooperative bank, with him as its head. Later, he promotes the idea of selling pieces of ("shares" in) individual producers, forming an exchange on which these shares can be bought and sold, with a levy on every transaction going to him, the entrepreneurial spirit who created and manages it all.

As time passes, this middleman becomes more and more sophisticated in his offerings and dealings, finding reason to charge a small fee for this and to take a small slice for that, like "the house" in Las Vegas coming out ahead, whether it rains or shines. With each extension and new offering, our by-now central character grows in influence and power. Having made himself an integral part of every transaction in the complicated system of exchange he authored and maintains, while producing nothing, he has gained the leverage to squeeze all the participants in the fair, and he uses it, ensuring that the lion's share no longer flows toward the producers but to himself and his selected cronies. He uses the laws that he has developed to protect himself and to strangle all those who object. Being the one with the most power, he is widely perceived as "the man."

Obviously, over time, this role of the "necessary" manager has expanded to include numerous and specialized nonproducing middlemen, especially banks, brokerage houses, insurance companies, reinsurance companies, and large law firms. The latest evolution of this self-feeding process is the proliferation and frenzied activity of private equity and hedge funds, which, in addition to making huge bets on things like commodity and currency swings, pool together enormous sums of borrowed money to take public companies private. Then, for a fixed fee and 20 percent of the profit, they often—if not usually—lay off workers, cut costs ruthlessly, sell off divisions to others who cut costs and lay off workers, repackage the company, and take it public again. All of this is allowed to happen with the glad assent of the banks, brokerage firms, and insurance companies which, also for a fee, use depositors' funds to participate in what is called improving efficiency. Little more than a scheme, the whole enterprise was concocted solely to line the pockets of those who fleece an unsuspecting public.

This is how middlemen, originally employed to provide needed services, have used their superior educations and brainpower over time to become legalized bandits. They don't wear masks, and only "their people" carry guns, but they certainly, in their reverse-Robin-Hood approach to life, rape, plunder, and pillage the unsuspecting and the poor. And because it pays so well, many of our brightest young people have traded their earlier dedication to idealism in for a fresher aspiration: a position in finance on Wall Street or Canary Wharf. Their hopes now rest in what they believe four houses filled with things and servants may offer.

And this is what, in gross terms, our friendly little crossroads fair has evolved into: a mechanism used by the clever for the betrayal of the public trust.

The Dairy Farm

In simple terms, heartless schemes are developed by hardhearted people, and modern companies are merely a reflection of the greediness in all of us. You may think of your place of business as a realm of reasonable commerce where you go to work, are appreciated for what you do, and reap rewards commensurate to your good efforts. In fact, your company, like most others, is likely more akin to a dairy farm than a field of honest endeavor. It is a place where you go regularly to be milked and milked again until one day, perhaps, you climb high enough to become a "milker." Yet even then, no matter how grand the title conferred upon you, unless you become one of the few with the power to skim the milk, you will be no more than just one of "the help," being milked for all you are worth, while used to furiously milk others.

If all of this sounds duplicitous and cold, that is because it is. Today, the once benign owners of the farms, now cleverly misnamed "the firms," are reacting to the shearing they experienced at the hands of middlemen by hiring uncaring "experts" to do the same to others, giving them the mandate to maximize current profits, to slash and burn, no matter the cost to the workers. Therefore these experts see you, sorry to say, as just one more side of beef, which is also exactly how the owners of the farms view them.

In this scheme you will be fed, of course, and at times, depending on your production, fed well. Yet do not slip into the weak-minded notion that this means someone cares for you personally or will even remember your present efforts if you falter and fall below average. You are being nourished now for the sole purpose of increasing your output, to maximize the amount of "milk" you, or your department, division, or company, produces. Frankly speaking, if you believe that you mean anything more to the owners of the farm than the value of your milk production, meat, hide, hooves, and tallow, you are perceiving things as you wish them to be, not as they are.

Want a Friend? Get a Dog

While all this may seem immaterial to one who thinks of himself as a professional manager, a financier, or an investor, it is not. Those who believe that the end (increasing profit) justifies the means (unfairness), and that there will be no reverberating cost for their duplicity, are mistaken. There is always a price to be paid for cruelty. It may be hidden, but it is always there. And now, unfortunately, the cruelty of business seems to be everywhere.

Take that paragon of business General Electric. Here is a company that excels at, among other things, avoiding taxes and social responsibility, yet is hailed as a paradigm of efficiency to be studied and emulated. Few firms can match its record of buying companies and slaughtering jobs, and few are as adept at convincing others that this murderousness is a sign of good management.

Buying growth, however, is not necessarily a sign of good management. Far too often the act is nothing more than an accounting sleight of hand, a way to seem to shine. Acquisitions are always wrapped around the acquired company's hidden problems whose eventual bite will be offset later by other accounting tricks, such as write-offs, or more acquisitions and slaughter. The vaunted "increased productivity" that is to come from acquisitions also is often a lie and simply means that the same amount of work is being done by fewer and fewer people. The result? The constant downward spiral of exceeding lowered expectations, and not much more.

As General Electric went on its rampageous way, it had in its corner that renowned gladiator Jack Welch. Christopher Byron in *Testosterone Inc.*, recounts when Welch took over GE:

> With the whole of the corporation now in his grasp, Welch did exactly what his performance had anticipated, initiating a Reign of Terror that wiped out 40,000 jobs in the first nine months and slashed another 60,000 … in the following two years…. Few areas of the country suffered more than the mid-Hudson River Valley of New York State and western Massachusetts….
>
> As the regional economy began to implode, "Out of Business" signs began appearing in store windows of one town after the next. After that came the drug trafficking and the gang violence, and the spread of burglaries…. GE had been the linchpin of the region's economy for generations, and its departure had come so abruptly and convulsively that people were simply overwhelmed by the resulting devastation….
>
> Jack … filed a financial … statement in October 2002 showing that his net worth consisted of roughly $440 million.[1]

Welch had a soul brother in "Chainsaw" Al Dunlap, whom Scott Paper hired. Again, from *Testosterone Inc.*:

> Lippincott [the previous manager] had already announced plans to cut Scott [Paper]'s workforce

by an unheard of 25 percent, letting go more than 8,300 employees over the following three years. What CEO wanted to preside over a blood-letting of that magnitude?

Answer: Chainsaw Al!... What Scott Paper got was Al Dunlap, human chainsaw. Lippincott's plan had been to cut the payroll by 8,300 over three years, but Big Al added 9,600 more to the hit list and chainsawed every one of them during his first eight months on the job.

"Rambo In Pinstripes," gushed the *Wall Street Journal*, awestruck at Dunlap's apparent success in pulling off "one of the fastest turnarounds in corporate history." His secret? According to the *Journal*, the winning formula boiled down to "clear vision, charisma, and decisive leadership."

In fact, Al's eviscerating chainsaw had sent Scott's business into a tailspin, causing operating cash flow ... to plunge by a third in 1994.... By the third quarter of 1995 ... cash flow fell into the red ... spelling the company's eventual doom.

Dunlap's compensation deal ... wound up putting roughly $100 million in his pocket.

When critics of his tactics brought up squishy questions like company morale or labor relations, Al just fired back with "Want a friend?... Get a dog!"[2]

This may sound like a harsh way to speak of businesspeople and their normal day-to-day activities, but is it? Looked at closely, are the hits in these examples all that different in their effects from the violence we condemn elsewhere? Does a psychological wound hurt less than a physical one? Does the shattering of a family's status quo feel all that different whether it comes from a crime, an accident, or an abrupt discharge? Is the result of cold-heartedness less painful than a kick or a punch or a battle wound?

In fact, emotional scars often take a longer time to disappear than physical ones.

The rationales for bloodletting business activity are well known: "It's for the good of the company," "We have to or we will fall behind the times," and so on. So, suppose GE, for example, fell a little behind the times and became a better example of corporate responsibility. Suppose Jack Welch had worked extra hard to figure out how to lay off 60,000 people instead of 100,000. If so, 40,000 families would have faced one less significant threat in their lives, and Mr. Welch and the large shareholders of GE would have made a little less money.

Voltaire put it this way: "It is forbidden to kill. Therefore, all murderers are punished, unless they kill in large numbers and to the sound of trumpets."[3] In corporate terms, this is what is seen as the right to lead tens of thousands of jobs to the slaughterhouse as we march "forward," faithfully serving the wildly victorious army of the god of profit.

As for business in general, obviously I do not believe that it, with its beloved mantra of free trade, is the grand answer to the travails of the world that it keeps proclaiming itself to be. In my opinion, it is all little more than a zero-sum game of energy transference between companies and people within companies, a divisive and debilitating game in which the strong grow stronger at the expense of the weak.

And despite what most business managers may believe, in this game of energy theft, no one, including the takers, really wins. When energy (i.e., capital) is drained from an organization through unfair means—meaning when the shareholders, financiers, or upper hierarchy of the company line their pockets at the expense of the laborers—the atmosphere and sustenance necessary for healthy growth is replaced by the sickness of guilt in the minds of the perpetrators and by the problem of debt in the companies.

This approach to business has taken such a pervasive hold in our society that debt is now perceived as welcome and, in some cases, even healthy. Likewise, and equally upside-down, holding cash has become an invitation to be taken over and plundered. Despite these deliberately shortsighted and self-serving notions, debt is not healthy over the long run, even when it is paid back with inflated dollars. But debt is especially not healthy when it is the result of strength having been sucked from the marrow of the organization.

In a system so radically skewed to favor those in power, long-range prosperity for all is a myth. And in this modern game of survival of the fittest, it is often the most cunning who thrive and not the fittest at all. Clearly, the gene pool of American industry is not being strengthened by the exploitive behavior of those who rule in such a system.

The way it works is that every business hawk or venture capitalist is convinced that borrowing is good, because he just "knows" he can earn more on the capital he borrows than the interest he is being charged. In turn, every bank, insurance company, and financial institution that cooperates with these characters just knows it can make more money from the fees and interest it charges them than the amounts it will have to pay to its depositors or bond or policy holders. That they are all gambling with your money is hidden from sight.

Marching in concert with these forms of taking advantage is the unbelievably accommodating Federal Reserve. The enemy of the prudent and the uninformed, this organization has for years done the mealy-mouthed two-step with presidents, politicians, and CEOs to keep the home fires of corporations and banks burning through theft of capital from people such as seniors living on interest income who are unable to protect themselves. In all of this, the Reserve and its cohorts have exhibited a blatant disregard of the "negative inheritance" of debt now being left to future generations.

Thomas Jefferson said, "We may consider each generation as a distinct nation, with a right, by the will of its majority, to bind themselves, but none to bind the succeeding generation, more than the inhabitants of another country."[4] Jefferson's advice is, to say the least, being ignored by the proponents of debt who continue to escape the consequences of their actions by consolidating current deficits and then turning them into longer-term obligations to be paid by future generations. But in this coterie of dissemblers' version of what they are doing, it is solely for the common good.

This is propaganda, lies told to maintain the status quo, because everyone is afraid of the fundamental changes an honest appraisal would require. So failed policies, which hurt the minds of the policy-makers as much as the lives of those seen as necessarily suffering collateral damage, are perpetuated in the name of this greater good. Surely there is no goodness in this approach to solving financial problems, no matter how loud and repetitive the claims to the contrary. How can the good be served by hurting the helpless?

This is the reality of the world of big business and finance today: it is designed to provide for the exploitation of the many for the benefit of the few, and the only way to survive in the bloody affair is to face that fact without shrinking.

A Common Problem

The game of big business is similar to the game of war, and that similarity is reflective of our common problem: we damage ourselves by maltreating others. One example of personal maltreatment comes from the book *Cold Storage* by Pulitzer Prize-winning journalist Wendell Rawls Jr. about life in Farview State Hospital, a mental institution near Philadelphia, the city of brotherly love.

"We heard horror stories of continuous beatings of patients with implements such as blackjacks and brass knuckles, as well as guards hitting and punching them unmercifully....

"Usually the patient was left there after in his injured condition with no medical attention to die a painful death. We have continuously found evidence of torn livers, punctured lungs, broken ribs, ruptured spleens and the like."[5]

What about torture stories from the Mafia; the Bataan Death March, where men were buried alive (of the 72,000 who started, only 7,500 survived); the Holocaust (13 million dead); and Nanking (300,000 dead); and the reports of millions more deaths in Rwanda, Cambodia, Sudan, Bosnia; and in our own Civil War. And the end of deaths in Iraq has not even been approached. These countless statistics can make one's eyes glaze over, or even shut.

The citation of man's inhumanity to man begs the questions, What about you? And what about me? Are we all that different from those who act on their careless, if not murderous, thoughts about others? Years ago, when I first started to pay attention to my thinking and honestly examine it, something surprised me. Every time I watched reports on television about a disaster in the nation, something like a hurricane or a flood, my first thought was never for the suffering victims, but rather how it would affect our sales in that area. It was a completely selfish outlook.

To look on my thoughts in such a way, without rationalizing, isn't being pessimistic, but realistic. Quite simply, society and business are the products of our individual mindsets, so there is no sense in bemoaning their state without first doing something about our own.

Here are some examples that show this problem is evident everywhere and in everyone. One of my daughters told me that when she was two, she used to take her baby brother's bottle and stick her thumb in his mouth while she drank it. One of my grandsons, when he was about two, responded to my stopping him from doing something by turning and puckering to spit at me, until he saw it was me and the look I was giving him. When I was four, my father hurt his leg at work. Later that evening, I jumped on him, and on his leg, in an exuberant burst of "affection." But was it? On my first day of school in the Bronx, when the teacher left the room for a minute, one boy rushed another from behind.

When the second boy's twin brother yelled "Duck!" and he did, the first boy flew over him, landing on the floor, with splinters all over his chin. He cried and the entire class laughed. Later that week the twins took me home with them after school. One of them had an argument with an older brother, and as I stood back and watched in amazement, the older brother chased him around a table, not just trying to catch him, but to stab him with a pair of scissors.

My reason for citing these examples of childhood perversity is to help you avoid misconstruing my diatribe against business as finger-pointing from a holier-than-thou attitude. The point I want to make is not just that business is hardhearted, or that we all—even two-year-olds—have a penchant for violence, but that there is no getting away with it.

Consider this recent come-on for visiting what is otherwise known as Sin City: "What happens in Vegas stays in Vegas," the ads seductively proclaim. No, it doesn't! What happens in Vegas stays in the person's mind until he or she finds a way to release it. The logical alternative, be it in Vegas or anywhere else, is to resist the siren call to hurt yourself by doing something you will regret later.

To look away from this common problem is simply denial. Saying it can't be that bad or that it doesn't apply to you will not make it go away; on the contrary, it will only drive the problem underground, making it that much harder to resolve later, when it will inevitably be forced to resurface.

Simply put: *The world is the way it is because we are the way we are, not the other way around.*

Living in a Wonderland Called More

In a deep examination of business, it is not difficult to perceive in its rituals, language, dress, and compounding rules and regulations an almost religious form of institutional insanity. Its vain pursuits and mean-spirited meanderings provide the underlying order to most of its up-and-down days. Looked upon with open eyes, business is reminiscent of the following excerpt from Lewis Carroll's *Alice's Adventures in Wonderland:*

> "In that direction," the Cat said, waving its right paw round, "lives a Hatter: and in *that* direction," waving the other paw, "lives a March Hare. Visit either you like: they're both mad."
>
> "But I don't want to go among mad people," Alice remarked.
>
> "Oh, you can't help that," said the Cat: "We're all mad here. I'm mad. You're mad."
>
> "How do you know I'm mad?" said Alice.
>
> "You must be," said the Cat, "or you wouldn't have come here."[6]

For our purposes, "wouldn't have come here" can be translated into "stayed for so long," and Wonderland as the incoherent, superficial competition for more, more, and then more. I know, you know, and somewhere inside themselves Big Al, Jack, and the rest of them know that replacing capital with debt and draconian cuts are improper, even though it is maximum slaughter that leads to maximum gain. But gain what, when you already have tens and hundreds of millions of dollars? More?

In *American Mania—When More Is Not Enough*, Peter C. Whybrow, M.D., the director of the Semel Institute for Neuroscience and Human Behavior at UCLA, says:

> In our search for happiness, we must look beyond the simple pursuit of material affluence....
>
> Our discovery that the challenges of the Fast New World have a disorganizing power over our physiological and mental well-being is knowledge too dangerous to ignore.... When neurobiology reminds us that as a species we are pleasure seekers and prone to addiction ... it is useful knowledge. Similarly, it is

valuable to learn that … the empathy … that brings happiness … requires a sympathetic culture in which to be expressed.…

Despite evidence that humans are prone to addiction and confused by abundance, as a culture we persist in exploiting desire and competition as the principal engines of "progress," offering little reward for social responsibility.…

Why do we live this way in a land where we are free to choose? [7]

Perhaps a few lines from Sigmund Freud, who kept insisting that uncovering the dark side of human nature was the only way to transcend it, will shed further light on our common problem. From his *Introductory Lectures on Psychoanalysis*:

Do you not know that all the transgressions and excesses of which we dream at night are daily committed in real life by waking men? And what does psychoanalysis do here but confirm Plato's old saying that the good are those who are content to dream of what the others, the bad, really do?

Think of the vast amount of brutality, cruelty and lies which are able to spread over the civilized world. Do you venture in such circumstances to break a lance on behalf of the exclusion of evil from the mental constitution of mankind?[8]

In other words, this problem is not unique to a few, as can be seen in the following frank account of the way things are in war and the way they were in Vietnam. This from *A Rumor of War* by former Marine Lieutenant Philip Caputo:

The fighting had not only become intense, but more vicious. Both we and the Viet Cong began to make a habit of atrocities.… There might have been more survivors had the Viet Cong not made a systematic massacre of the wounded....

We paid the enemy back, sometimes with interest. It was common knowledge that quite a few captured VC never made it to prison camps.... Some line companies did not even bother taking prisoners; they simply killed every VC they saw, and a number of Vietnamese who were only suspects.

Everything rotted and corroded quickly over there: bodies, boot leather, canvas, metal, morals.... Our humanity rubbed off us as the protective bluing rubbed off the barrels of our rifles.... It was ... a war for survival waged in a wilderness without rules or laws; a war in which each soldier fought ... not caring who he killed ... or how many or in what manner and feeling only contempt for those who sought to impose on his savage struggle the mincing distinctions of civilized warfare—that code of battlefield ethics that attempted to humanize an essentially inhuman war....

Finally, there was hatred, a hatred buried so deep that I could not then admit its existence. I can now, though it is still painful. I burned with a hatred for the Viet Cong and with an emotion that dwells in most of us, one closer to the surface than we care to admit: a desire for retribution.... Revenge was one of the reasons I volunteered [to go back to] a line company. I wanted to kill somebody.[9]

What Passes Cannot Be All That Important

As for the expression of this problem in big business, its darkest side becomes clearest in its continuing carelessness about the damage it may do to people's lives. Here is an example from *Barron's* (June 2004) in which the president of Zulauf Asset Management gives his reasons to own shares of Fiat, the Italian automaker:

Things have changed due to the death of Fiat's chairman…. The new CEO … formerly was the head of Alusuisse, which he merged into Pechiney…. He has never been long in a job—two or three years at most. He gets a nice option plan and gets the stock price up. Either he merges the company or sells it or creates some sort of turnaround that lasts for a few years….

In the next six months (the stock) could run to 10 and you could make 50% on your money. But I wouldn't invest for five years; I'm not sure the company will make it.[10]

That well may be a realistic assessment of the situation, and Mr. Zulauf's business is stock-picking, not management, so I have no quarrel with his advice, but he is in essence lauding the new CEO of Fiat for his track record as a robber baron.

This makes no sense for the company or its employees, who are seen as pawns to be shoved aside or out. Yet the most common oversight in this scheme is that it equally makes no sense for the perpetrators. Through such actions, their sensitivity becomes so calloused that they no longer recognize that what causes them pain is not the world, but their "I couldn't care less" attitudes toward others.

If every attack on another has an equal and opposite psychological reaction on the attacker in the form of regret, either conscious or unconscious, then those who seek to do harm are, without exception, functioning in a state of unawareness. In other words, no one consciously puts his hand on a hot stove, and if he does, he knows why it hurts afterward. Yet highly placed and otherwise rational businesspeople regularly lay their minds in beds of hot coals through egregiously selfish actions and then wonder why their sleep is disturbed or their marriage in flames.

The hallmarks of the successful businessperson in our society have become action, deals, money, self-centeredness, excitement, distraction, overcoming, doing, and never resting. "I'm late, I'm late, for a very important date." "Surely

I am important. I received 120 e-mails yesterday." "My two cell phones never stop ringing." "I need an assistant for my assistant." "My work is very serious. The family will just have to wait. After all, I am doing this for them, am I not?" "This task must be completed. It has major ramifications for everyone." "Sorry, guys, this is vital; everyone is going to have to work again this weekend."

The intensity, the action, and the worry all gather to give the perception of a successful person. Often, unfortunately, such a perception begins with parents. When I was in grammar school, a bright boy who lived a block or so away invited me home to do homework with him. It was winter and his mother put us in a warm corner, gave us cookies, and started us on our way. We did homework and more homework. When it was time for us to go outside for playtime, she had us do more homework and then even more. She was a very nice lady, but even at that age, I could see she was madly ambitious for her son, deadly serious about ensuring he did better than others. As for him, he got great grades, but he never learned to play ball, or for that matter, how to play at all. As for me, I never went back.

Almost all who dedicate themselves wholly to outdo become consumed by the attempt. If they are overly religious, they often become self-righteous; if they are military zealots, they usually need an enemy; if they are businesspeople, they normally live for the deal. Self-importance flows from their pores. And, despite all my cautions, for a long time I thought just like them. I remember walking up the fourth fairway of a golf course, telling a friend about my plans to leave that evening for a vacation in London. I realized only later that half the reason I chose to go to a place I had been so many times before was to proclaim to him and to others that I was off to London again.

If you are as entangled as I was in the delusion that what you do is very important, you do not yet perceive that anything that is passing cannot be particularly significant. If it is not that significant, it cannot be that serious. If it is not all that serious, it is not really a big deal. If it is not any of these things, how can worrying about it help you to become Mr. Serious? Or Mr. Big Deal?

While on the surface it may seem absurd to suggest that certain people would want their problems to be of a serious nature, so that others would see them as serious characters, many often do just that. So uncertain of where satisfaction lies, they settle for a life of contending seriously with the past, present, and future, because what else would the serious do?

The Thief of Tranquility

Another debilitating outcome of an unwitting investment in self-importance is a desperate need to be in control of events. This usually leads to forming preconceptions about outcomes. The more the investment in such, the more exacting the toll if things turn out unexpectedly.

When something or someone fails you and you get upset about it, it is you, not it or they, who is missing the mark. Disappointment is caused by an error in perception on your part, not by the person or event that seems to be its cause. Without the confusion engendered by preconceptions, you would recognize only the positive side of disappointment. This is the side that suggests you free yourself from the real problem: your insistence that things or people be different. Without opposition, events and others are allowed to be what they are, no longer disappointing, just what they are.

Let's say you have just returned to your office after a long road trip and are hoping for a day or two of relative calm. Just as you begin to settle back in, the boss comes in and says, "Sorry, but we have an emergency at the main plant, and I need you in Pittsburgh first thing in the morning. You can catch the seven o'clock flight tonight, and Fowler will meet you at the airport. See you when you get back."

Now, while this is reasonably polite, it is also, like much of business, inconsiderate. The boss could have added, for example, "I'm well aware of how tired you must be, and I'll make it up to you later." Or he could have said, "Tell your wife and children I'm sorry to drag you away again like this, but it is a serious problem and we do need you there." He might even have said, "I will not let this happen again for a while." But he did not.

In such a circumstance, it is likely that at least part of your mind will leap up in resentment and begin something like this lament: "Here I am, exhausted after a long trip, having worked hard and done my very best. And no one can go to Pittsburgh except me? What kind of a one-sided, lousy deal is this, anyway? I feel just about used and abused enough to pack it in. Right is right and wrong is wrong, and this is *so* wrong." And on and on such "poor me" thinking goes.

Where does this kind of angry response come from? Obviously, despite the inconvenience, this assignment in itself is not a big deal. You have done things like this numerous times before. Yet you find yourself resisting, making it difficult to release yourself from your negative interpretations of what is being asked of you. Why? Because you drifted into unawareness and left your mind unguarded, allowing that thief of tranquility called preconception to enter, plant itself, and take root. Because you unknowingly formed a picture of your day at work on your terms, and the boss came in and took your picture away.

Where is the real problem in this situation? Is it in the directive you received or in the way you are choosing to look at the scenario? If the problem is what showed up without your permission, you are in big trouble, not only in this event, but in everything unexpected that you deem unjust. On the other hand, by being aware that the problem was caused by your own preconception, you can remember your power to change your mind and decide to let go of the issue. Doing so might even lead you to realize that you can make such a choice anytime you want.

This step of awareness allows you to realize that you have a new frontier to conquer (i.e., your mind), and then empowers you to decide to meet this goal in the business setting. Now, instead of using instances of disappointment to complain about what seems unfair, you can use them to watch your thinking, becoming a more honest witness to what you may actually be up to.

When you consider such a shift in thinking seriously, you start to realize that you can do two things at once. You can develop the ability to watch the storms of upset within your mind rise and fade away, and all the while, you can function efficiently. It takes willingness and practice, but it can be accomplished. And it is an option that is much more helpful than speaking your childish mind or becoming so enchanted with the idea of unfairness that you can no longer think logically.

In his book *I Call the Shots*, the professional golfer—now announcer—Johnny Miller wrote the following about this idea of doing two things at once:

> **Golf Announcing 101**
> **Rule No. 1: Learn to talk and listen at the same time.** These headsets we wear in the booth get a workout. In the organized confusion that reigns during a broadcast—particularly if it's Sunday afternoon and there's a crowded leader board—voices are chattering in your ear constantly. And it isn't idle chatter. You're informed of what's going on out on the course, asked to comment on something, or told where the action is going next. The trick is to talk intelligently while listening to the director at the same time. Some experts say the mind can only concentrate on one thing at a time, but I don't believe it. You can learn to describe verbally what you're seeing while at the same time gathering the important fragments of what someone else is saying.[11]

Here is my version of the same idea:

> **Rule #1: Learn to talk and watch your mind at the
> same time.** Your inner "ears" will get a workout. In the
> unorganized confusion that reigns during every mental
> storm, particularly if it's about a subject you believe
> is serious, the thoughts of unfairness are chattering
> constantly, but it is all idle chatter. It only informs
> you of the version of reality formulated by your self-
> importance, usually demanding that you verbally lash
> out or take this or that hostile action. The trick is to
> learn to talk intelligently, while watching the internal
> storm as it rolls on by. Some experts say the mind can
> only concentrate on one thing at a time, but don't you
> believe it. You can learn to deal calmly with what you
> are seeing *and* the upset in your mind, without giving
> either the power to direct your life.

Thinking Makes It So

A quote in Shakespeare's *Hamlet* says, "There is nothing either good
or bad but thinking makes it so."[12] It is important to understand
that this is applicable to everything, but especially to how you see
yourself in relationship to others.

When I was quite young, a family with money and seeming
prominence came to visit my parents a few times. What their
connection or reason for visiting was I do not know, but they came
with two daughters, and I grew to like the younger one. When
I expressed my feelings to my mother, she, in a nice way and
without being overly explicit, tried to discourage me, intimating
that we were of different classes, that the girl was, if you will, out
of my league. While I understand now that my mom was trying
to prevent me from being hurt, fortunately, I didn't buy into such
beliefs, then or later. And while I could not have expressed it
this way then, now I see it as the other side of the coin of self-

importance: self-degradation or staying put in your "assigned" place.

Once, years later, I had lunch with a multibillionaire at his New York townhouse, along with an ex-secretary of state, an ex-first lady, a few business tycoons, and some other notables. I was younger than most of them, nowhere nearly as well-known as any of them, and probably poorer than all of them. But I certainly didn't feel out of my league, or even that the luncheon meant anything in particular. They were all just people, even if well-known, and the lunch was just lunch, albeit in a grand setting. It was simply what it was, and how I felt about it, just as how I'd felt about liking that "higher-class" girl, came fully from me, and not from the situation.

What Shakespeare was saying in *Hamlet* is just that: everything, business included, is neither good nor bad, but up to your interpretation. Learning that this is so will help you enormously. It will help you begin to relax. Then what happens, happens, and you deal with it, after which you wait quietly for the next matter, and nothing more—or less.

As soon as you recognize that nothing is overly important until you make it so, your power to deal impersonally with whatever comes will transform threatening situations into energy for your transformation, changing all that seemed negative in the big, bad world into something positive for you.

2
The Good

The Only Freedom

The good in big business is that, despite its wicked ways, the employment it provides has much to contribute to your well-being.

Work well-executed, regardless of outcome, has great value. Not because of the work itself, but because of what you can learn from it. At an early stage in your career, it may seem as though the work tells you what you are in relation to it. But in fact, it is exactly the other way around: the situation reflects your own thinking back to you. Therefore, in relationship to your well-being, the fact that the game is slanted in another's favor means nothing. Crooked or legitimate, it has the power to teach you about yourself, and in a world of confusion such as ours, *nothing* is more important than that.

In his book *The First and Last Freedom,* Krishnamurti says that facing what is uncomfortable in our thoughts and relationships rewards us with self-knowledge, something we all should consider carefully:

What will bring peace is inward transformation, which will lead to outward action. Inward transformation is not isolation, is not a withdrawal from outward action. On the contrary, there can be right action only when there is right thinking and there is no right thinking where there is no self-knowledge. Without knowing yourself there is no peace.[13]

Looking at yourself without self-deception is critical. When I was quite young, I decided to seek friendship with a strong, popular boy in our class, not because I cared for him, but because I hoped it would do something positive for my image. Having nothing in particular to offer him—in trade, you might say—I decided to "reach him" by befriending one of his friends. Fortunately, before I assaulted my character too much, I realized what I was doing, got disgusted with myself, and stopped.

The value of honesty in such situations—and life is filled with uncomfortable opportunities of this sort—is to see the value in learning about our minds and then to act on that value by paying attention to ourselves in every relationship. When we were kids, we used to say, "Sticks and stones will break my bones, but names will never hurt me." While this is true, it is also true that we don't believe it. We give names, the opinions of others, even our own beliefs, great power, and we often fall into conflicts with others because of them. One of the more important things you will discover in this objective appraisal of yourself is that no one has the power to belittle you unless you have *first* belittled yourself. Without self-condemnation to rebound from, the mistakes and slanders of others have no place to gain a foothold and, therefore, no effect on you.

Dr. Kenneth Wapnick, president of the Foundation for *A Course in Miracles* and on the current scene of wise men—in my opinion, the wisest of them all—has an interesting way of expressing this same idea, and then taking it one step further.

He says that: "If you perceive hostility in another and you react to it, the hostility is in you." He follows with: "The other may have attack thoughts, but what does that possibly have to do with you?"[14]

A Positive Outlook

Business is also the perfect place to learn that success as you presently know it is always trailed by the shadow of the fear of failure and, therefore, is not real success at all. That's because real success cannot be found in a "winning" that includes a potential for loss; rather, it can only be found in the freedom that lies beyond winning and losing alike.

As you consider this idea, understand that real success requires that you deal with the fearful opinions that well up in you during stressful situations as the matador deals with the bull: not through confrontation or denial, but by a graceful stepping aside. One of the greatest challenges in life is to learn to pay careful attention to the presence of these doubtful voices, but none to what they say.

In addition, to succeed at work while both winning and losing requires adopting the mindset not only of bullfighters, but of good card players. Like them, you play not for occasional fits of excitement, but to survive. This requires that you give long-range thinking priority in your mind and that you *never* perceive a current gain that will be trailed by a long-term loss to be acceptable or even attractive.

Over the long haul, the majority of career-builders meet up with about the same number of ups and downs and are dealt about the same mix of cards. What makes the successful players different from the rest? First of all, they are aware that while there will be occasion for bold movement, there is no place for recklessness in business, where victory is won in a burst of glorious action by the hero of the game. Are these successful businesspeople gamblers at times? Yes. But mostly, they are simply people who play the odds while keeping their attitude positive, because this attitude is the most important contributor to minimizing unavoidable damage and maximizing potential gain.

Without a clear-cut positive outlook, reinforced regularly, it is impossible to see clearly enough to recognize the end of a downturn and the beginning of a new trend. And only when you see clearly do you know when to bet and when to hedge, when to assume prudent risk and when to sit out the hand.

A different way to say this is that when your common sense, which often expresses itself as gut feelings, tells you not to force the issue and to wait for a more opportune moment to proceed, listen to it, and, even if small losses ensue, be patient. Remember, it is not necessary to win every hand to win the game.

Acting Against Your Conditioning

Business is a game that mimics war, and in that sense, business is no more complicated than any other kind of competition. You will learn from studying history that "divide and conquer" is a solid strategy for winning battles. In business, this strategy equates to dividing up tasks, prioritizing them appropriately, and then conquering them one by one.

Every business life well-lived is founded on the cornerstone of listing, impersonally and continuously, problems in a descending order of importance and then tackling the toughest first. To ensure success in this, you must:

- Begin with a proper definition of the problem.
- Carefully review its proposed resolution.
- Check regularly on the progress of the problem's undoing.
- Maintain an uncompromising attitude toward its final dissolution.

The effective methodology that accompanies such actions is being in touch with the work, remaining connected to both your instincts and your company's monitoring systems, and pausing the moment you sense something is discordant. Only when you become sensitive enough to feel the underlying flow of the work can you be truly effective, because only then do you become consistently alert for problems and their proper disposition.

As you grow in competence and have less need to dwell on the mechanics of business and more time to focus on how your mind functions on the battlefield, you will begin to realize there is much more to life than can ever be found in success, promotions, or gain in the marketplace. It's hard to accept this fully at first, because we are conditioned by our educational and athletic activities, by fearful or ambitious parents, by books and movies, and so on, to worship getting ahead above all. Yet the reality is that to go to the office day after day *only* to work, marching in lockstep as just another robot, makes for a monstrous life and a very dull mind.

Yes, it is true that you must work to feed yourself, and, yes, you may have to contend with the following:

1. Business is a man's game.
2. Your best friend does not always understand you.
3. Your mother is not always kind.
4. Minorities are sometimes discriminated against.
5. Some days you feel horrible.
6. The most qualified person does not always get the job.
7. Your body does not always function perfectly.
8. Your boss is not unfailingly appreciative.
9. A number of people in the world are more intelligent than you are.
10. You may not end up with an inheritance.
11. There are those who dislike you without cause.
12. The world is not always fair.

But what does any of this have to do with learning about yourself or laying the foundation for a sound career?

Your perceptions about some roadblocks you encounter at work will have a measure of truth to them. Your perceptions about others will not. A man rejected your idea because, say, you are a woman and he needs to be dominant. Perhaps that's true. Or a woman rejected your idea because you are a man and she needs to be dominant. Perhaps that's true. Or a man rejected your idea because you are bright and new ideas threaten him. Perhaps. On the other hand, perhaps the idea was odious. Or maybe the idea was good, but your presentation was inadequate or unconvincing. Or, possibly, the idea needed further development or conflicted with plans of which you were unaware.

The biggest roadblocks you will encounter in business, however, are internal, the ones that lead you to believe that because you know some things, you know a lot. One of my early lessons with this came not in business but in a series of experiences that proved just how little I understood about investing. When I was in my mid-twenties and starting to make decent money, I worked with a large group of young men, a number of whom were heavily into the market. So I got in, too. I still can see myself as a young man, meeting early in the morning with the guys to discuss our latest hot tips, some of us, myself included, opening the *Wall Street Journal* to see how our stocks had closed, inch by inch, as if we were squeezing out a hand of cards. At that point the economy was good and the stock market was hot. We all made what was, for us at the time, serious money. I tripled my initial stake of $20,000 in little over a year. But then in the following two years, the market turned south and I lost over $100,000. After that, I tried a couple mutual funds that went nowhere and, still later, made a few investments on my own, the last and the largest in a stretch-fabric-producing company at $50 per share. I barely escaped at $20 per share before it sank out of sight.

As a memento of my severely impaired skills in this arena, I still have a worthless 10,000-share stock certificate of Ethyl Copper Company. The shares quadrupled and then hit oblivion before I could get my greedy, sticky hands off the investment.

I had the certificate framed and kept it on the wall for years to remind me that while I was smart enough about some things, I didn't understand the market at all.

How we ever got into such foolishness in the first place still puzzles me. I think it was because we got carried away by the excitement, a bunch of young fools with the unjustified notion that we were smarter than we were. The upside of the experience, however, is that it became a wonderful reminder of my occasional lapses into insensibility.

A Balanced Approach

The need to think sensibly should apply to every aspect of an ambitious person's business life. As your career flourishes, you will find it valuable to demand of yourself that you become responsible even in the smallest matters, and to insist that those who work for you accept that same sense of responsibility.

True, when you become a manager, it is your duty to be reasonable and fair, yet when an employee refuses to cooperate, you have an equal duty to be responsible enough to fire him. By the time the habitually uncooperative person gets fired from the second or third position, it should begin to dawn on him that he must have some part in the situation. This realization will be enough to help him crawl out of the swamp of excuses he surrounded himself with, leaving you, who fired him first, whether he realizes it or not, his friend.

Remember, it is not kind to be inappropriately considerate of people any more than it is fair to be unduly harsh. Only the irresponsible manager smothers someone who works for him with the saintly love he believes he has for the downtrodden or, instead, sets the dogs on the dirty so-and-so. In *both* cases the manager looks down on the employee.

Think about it. How would such unbalanced responses feel to you? Probably insulting and unprofessional. Business is not personal; therefore, your relationships with those who work for you should be intelligently impersonal as well. This means that when fluctuating emotion rises up to interfere with your rational thinking, which, if you are paying attention, you will always find it doing after you have fired or demoted someone even when it is fully justified, the sensible answer is to tell it to take a hike.

Yet, go slowly before acting in the first place. When you are about to react to someone you have a problem with at work, the first and most important question to ask yourself is, "Would my doing this be helpful?" If you even suspect it would not, don't do it. If you are sure it would, act forthrightly. And if you are caught in the middle, wait. Sometimes the time for yes or no has just not arrived, while other times, because problems often solve themselves, waiting ends up meaning never having to act at all.

Remember, too, as you learn more about responsibility, that when it comes to your own work, it is your business to do your best and your supervisor's to grade those efforts as he or she sees fit. When the boss is dissatisfied and your grades are low, it is up to you to improve them by pleasing your supervisor in his or her requested fashion and not your own. Only a willingness to cooperate can overcome the resistance to authority many carry with them like a bad seed. Take this as gospel from one who learned this lesson firsthand.

We can all be pretty stubborn about things, yet stubbornness is not an ally in forging a successful career; flexibility is. By the same token, if your boss is often unreasonable and you have truly put forth your best effort and are still not met with fairness, then perhaps, but only perhaps, you should quit. Before you take such an important step, though, one that affects not only you, but your family, choose your next step carefully. First, try to accept that your main problem is always with your thinking and not with the actual situation, even if the boss has been less than encouraging. After all, if the arena is there so you can learn to play the slanted game in such a way that no matter what happens, you become stronger, who is proclaiming that this is unfairness except you?

Second, consider what is going on. Maybe the boss's lack of appreciation has been magnified by your own imagination. Maybe she is upset about a personal issue and, therefore, critical of everyone. Maybe it is time to go to your boss's boss and complain about your maltreatment. Maybe you face the somewhat uncomfortable but golden opportunity to seek a better job. Maybe you should start your own business. (If you choose this avenue, do your best to be certain it will lead to a business with a solid chance of success, not a wishful cop-out that will merely waste your time and money.) Maybe you should put forth an even greater effort to overcome your boss's lack of appreciation. Maybe you should simply resist the temptation to quit and remain patient for a while. Maybe you should quit next Monday.

Whatever you decide, honor it with everything at your disposal, especially when the snide whisperings of uncertainty come to insist you have gone astray. They will, and you haven't.

Knowing When to Stop

It is not easy to trust your deepest feelings and maintain a real sense of confidence. There is a certain strange attraction to the belief in a personal weakness, in being one more of those who cannot do for themselves. Yet many who at first succumb to this fallacy are the very people who, when they finally decide to stand up for themselves, discover they are not weak at all. This means that the real problem lies only in the sick belief and the weird attraction to it, never in the person. This also means that all who suffer from the sickness can do something about their "condition." They can begin to devalue the strange belief, and thus the sad attraction to it.

When I was a young salesman, charged with making quotas and succeeding at the tough job of making cold-canvass calls to sell word-processing and billing machines in midtown Manhattan, in my every weak moment I could not wait until I became a manager.

I wanted to share with others some of the burden of responsibility I felt so deeply. When I received my first promotion and then had five salespeople working for me, I felt relieved. Soon enough, however, I realized that I had not actually lightened my load but increased it. Now, while continuing to be responsible for myself, I had to add responsibility for the production of the other five people as well.

As I climbed the corporate ladder, right up until my career reached its pinnacle, and even afterwards, I accepted every assignment with this mindset: that I was responsible for the success of the assignment, for myself, and for the output of the people under me—whether five people or, at the end, thousands, it made no difference. There is no escape from the need to assume this mantle if you want to climb the corporate ladder. Such a climb is not easy, and it is almost impossible to accomplish without embracing not only the challenge of complete responsibility, but also, sometimes, even self-sacrifice. What I mean is that if you are good at what you do, sooner or later someone will notice and offer you more, and there will be a catch to that more. The catch is whatever the giver of the more wants in return. If you are ambitious, this catch is the price you must pay.

If you are successful in Ohio and they need help in Texas, that is where you will be expected to go. If you continue to be good at what you do, just about the time you and the family have settled down in Dallas, you will be asked to move to Atlanta or wherever you can serve the corporate interests best. When this happens, if you want to get ahead, in most cases, you go.

When I was young and excited about the game and the rewards it offered, I certainly wanted to get ahead. So, in one six-year stretch, I moved from New York to Northern California to Southern California to Connecticut to New York to Southern California to New York and back to Southern California. I wasn't happy with some of these assignments, but they were the roads that opened up to me, and, with the consent of my first wife, I took them.

When I landed back in Southern California for the third time, like a rolling stone that had found its place, I stopped. Over the years that ensued, I was offered a number of "better" jobs in New York and elsewhere, each of which I gracefully declined. I had found the place I wanted to live, I had climbed the corporate ladder, I was making more than enough money, and I had gained the wisdom to see that neither money nor position had any great meaning in itself, and, therefore, more of the same would just be more of the same.

3

The Practical

Eliminating the Unessential

Every company is like a family. Each has an income, expenses, savings, debts, responsibilities to its members, leaders, duties, and most of all, a common purpose. So what is the basic constitution of a stable, successful family? Does it have to do with the greatest success stories or the fewest problems, the best-known name or the hardest-working members, the grandest quarters, the fanciest pedigree, or the highest income? Not at all! The foundation stone of a successful family is that whatever happens, it cares for its members equally and completely. Can a company do less and remain successful over the long term?

Running a business effectively can also be compared to directing an orchestra: break down the general task into a number of specifics, give each specific to the musician with the right instrument and skill (i.e., education or experience, and attitude), promote from within the company the best-qualified person to be the conductor, teach him or her what to do, watch that person do it until you are sure he or she can do it competently, then do this time and again, and still again, always paying careful attention to the three major elements: the music, the musicians, and the conductor, and what you can do to improve them all.

Suppose for a moment that you were put in charge. What would your company end up looking like if, when you became the boss, you started afresh and you eliminated all the unessential and selfish practices that had crept in and did not serve the best interests of the whole? Consider the following eighteen practices, which I had to modify or eliminate in a company:

1. Overplanning

In business, the fundamental task does not lie in planning ahead, as so many believe, but in asking yourself each morning, "What am I going to do to improve the passion and the message of the music today?" Often this means trusting your common sense and just getting on with it, whatever the "it" may be.

A significant impediment to such effective action comes in organizations where managers are allowed to hide in long meetings, ponder problems academically, and then create and strictly enforce exacting rules. Being afraid to deal directly with the employees they manage and unwilling to shoulder their responsibility to encourage a feeling of safety about the arbitrary (mis)use of the rules, they become the very enemies they should be protecting their employees from. In their timidity, they conspire to develop "laws" to protect the status quo, telling themselves they do so *not* because they are fearful of the intensity required in human interaction, but for "the good of the company." The longer this is permitted to go on, the more they come to speak with a growing fervor about "our company's rules and regulations," and then finally "our traditions," all in a hidebound attempt to prevent the discomfort of change that all healthy companies must undergo in order to grow.

Overplanning and abiding by strict rules are exercises in futility. If you are a good businessperson, you are in touch with the employees and the business on a daily basis. You know the industry, the market, the potential, and the risks, as well as the attitudes of your people. You can "feel" the changes as well as see them, and you continuously adjust the business accordingly. When you operate this way, unseparated from the operations and directly in the thick of things, you do not plan—you act.

This is not to say that you should have no long-range plans; it just means they should not be set in concrete or laid out in endless detail. Those plans should not be your guide, but the product of your current estimations, and they should be easily adjustable. In short, they should be no more than just plans.

A big problem with overplanning is that it easily deludes you into thinking you can predict the future. The more you plan for the future in detail, the more deeply rooted your belief in that future becomes. So in overplanning, you can easily become rigid and thereby greatly hinder your ability to quickly abandon one course of action for another.

This happened to a good friend, the CEO of a medium-sized drug company whose main products were coming off patent and whose research and development had nothing particularly hot to offer. When I told him that I thought he should adopt the strategy of his enemies: stop worrying about what the generic drug companies were going to do to his company and combat their strategy by becoming one himself, he couldn't get unstuck from thinking this would be a slight to his company. So he didn't, and they ate his lunch and, later, his dinner. It wasn't necessary, but his fixed thinking made it so.

2. Underpricing and overreporting

In my company, I consistently looked at the least profitable 10 percent of the business and either successfully raised its pricing or let it go elsewhere. I did this to keep the pipelines through which the company's business flowed (the capital equipment and processing systems) clean, or freer. As a result, we were much more capable of processing efficiently the better-priced and more profitable work that was coming in, with the added benefit of constantly enriching the mix of the business. As part of this effort to become more effective, I also regularly required that all the major reports the company was producing be laid out on the conference room table. I would then ask the responsible parties what they were using the reports for, and, like the least-profitable business, weed out everything not current or vital.

Bureaucracies are strange creatures. They grow almost of their own volition, and sloppiness, overreporting, and unnecessary paperwork are the means that allow them to do so.

3. Interfering in communication

In my last company of about 7,500 people, there were no complicated telephone systems. Whoever wished to speak to me reached me directly. If I was already on the phone when another person called, I would ask the person I was speaking with to hold for a moment while I answered the other line. If the second caller needed a yes or no or wait answer, I gave it and was done. If the second caller needed more, I would promise to call back. I then quickly returned to the first call, said, "Sorry for the interruption," and continued. Every manager in the company was trained to do the same. Communication was free, brisk, and efficient. In addition, when I wanted to drop someone a note, I most often did so in a few words and by hand.

It seemed to me that the rest of it, like "push this button, and then that button, and then that button," along with typewritten letters or lengthy e-mails about little matters, was essentially time-wasting, formalized nonsense.

4. Hang-ups on form

Form for the sake of form contributes nothing to the bottom line. Dress codes beyond cleanliness and neatness are at best questionable. They often cause employees unnecessary expense and can easily lead to dressing competitions, when the focus should be on work competitions. Equally useless are rules of communication that insist on specific forms to be filled out for every grievance.

In our company, the policy was that if you had a problem, you went to your manager. If your manager could not solve the problem, you and the manager, without delay, went to the manager's manager. If that did not work, you had continued access up the line, eventually to me.

To ensure this open communication was effective, I formed an Employee Advocates department in headquarters, in which two highly qualified people did nothing all day but call managers to ask, "Are there any problems with the employees in your department we do not know about that should be addressed before they become bigger?" Our client services force, which numbered in the hundreds, did exactly the same thing by phone and in person with our clients. Both approaches reflected that old Walt Disney idea: "Wash the windows before they get dirty."

5. Embellishments

Every company needs stronger muscles, which lead to greater production. The fancy and the dainty and the baroque, while at times attractive, do not increase overall effectiveness. Clean, comfortable, secure, and quiet: these are the conditions that should be provided for everyone at work. All the rest is just meant to impress, leaving these questions: To impress whom? And for what reason?

6. Overly bureaucratic or outmoded rules

In our company, as I eliminated from the mix the least profitable business and the most underused reports, I also examined, with a critical eye, the rules by which we operated. Obviously rules, such as being on time, not having inappropriately excessive absences, speaking civilly, maintaining personal hygiene, doing your work, following safety standards, and proceeding through a normal chain of command, are required in any organization. Past that, many of the rules you find today are the products of people with an exaggerated sense of caution or without enough real work to do.

Because there are always some who refuse to participate in the common mission, rules are necessary. Rule-making is meant to bind the uncooperative in a framework that minimizes the damage they can do. Rules must not, however, be permitted to grow. This means that a company's set of regulations needs constant attention, care, deliberation, and pruning. Otherwise, it will slowly squeeze the entrepreneurial spirit of an organization like a boa constrictor squeezes the life out of its prey.

7. Unnecessary positions

I always believed it was the obligation of management not to enter into boom-and-bust cycles that meant employees were being added or subtracted in large numbers. I never bought into the idea that an exciting increase in this year's profit, followed by a scramble to make up for its absence later, made any sense, at least to someone who was planning to stick around for a while. I also did not subscribe to the callous idea of buying your competitors and paying for the purchase by eliminating positions in both companies. In addition to being opportunistic and heartless, such a practice is, at times, shortsighted and foolish. When you buy a competitor, you also buy its hidden problems. As a boss of mine once told me, "Two sick dogs do not make a well dog."

I am not against acquisitions, which sometimes make great sense, but I am against the concept as a strategy and a policy. It is always more profitable and less disturbing to the organization to train one's own troops to get up the gumption to go out and take the competitor's business away.

All of that said, however, within every company, unnecessary positions should be eliminated. Of course, this must be done carefully and, above all, fairly, but it is a part of business and therefore a boss's responsibility.

8. Idle luxuries

It is nonsense to believe that expensive, wine-soaked luncheons or dinners do anything beyond satisfying the desires of the participants who feast grandly on the company's money, justifying the expense because it is for business purposes—and tax-deductible to boot.

And even in the largest of companies, special rugs on the floor are no more required in the CEO's office than elsewhere. Huge offices, art on the walls, chandeliers and sculptures—all paid for out of the company's coffers—do nothing more than create a fantasy world wherein the hierarchy can proclaim their difference from the masses. Unfortunately, the fact that many in the hierarchy came directly from the masses seems out of their awareness now that they have arrived.

9. Special benefits for the elect

I am not against special treatment for the hierarchy; after all, their responsibility is far greater than that of the masses. But I have grown to be against excess. Those who take too much often get caught in wanting more and then grabbing more, which in turn teaches others to want more and to grab more too.

In addition, giving the elect special benefits can easily breed a false sense of importance, and those in the hierarchy who start believing in their own specialness instead of feeling increased loyalty toward the employees and gratitude for their better roles are misunderstanding their place.

So should the hierarchy be treated specially? If they have earned it, yes. But most of their special treatment should come in the form of direct remuneration, not in the secreted benefits they take but are ashamed to disclose.

10. Egregiously excessive salaries

Should top producers make top dollars? Yes. Does the potential for an unlimited income make for a better producer? Not necessarily. In straight commission sales, with a sensible monitoring of pricing and profitability, it can, and should; but elsewhere, egregious salaries for a select few add no great value. Instead, they often lead to resentment among those who make less.

11. Stock options

Obviously, excessive remuneration includes income from all sources, including options. I believe options are far less productive than commonly perceived. Is it really coincidental that both earnings and stock prices fell off the cliff at GE, IBM, Citigroup, Scott Paper, Sunbeam, and others like them not long after their chairmen left office? Is it possible that actions taken to keep the stock price up while they were still there were paid for dearly by others later?

Another problem with the extraordinary focus on options and today's stock price is that it inevitably feeds short-term thinking. How many people with options that expire soon will consider making a large investment that will not pay off until years in the future? Such factors are almost never taken into consideration at bonus and options times. If managers had less reason to focus on the market's reaction and the current stock price when making investment decisions about the future, there would be a much more practical approach to the problems and opportunities of any business.

The widely held belief that stock options make people feel like owners is also nonsense, in my opinion. Responsible people always feel, think, and act like owners; irresponsible people forever do not, and I believe options influence neither. Would I do away with all stock options? Yes.

12. Unreasonable financial protection for top executives only

It is reasonable for certain managers to have the protection of a contract, or preferably a severance agreement, just as it is reasonable to make decent and even generous severance policies available for laid-off employees. Yet the prime hidden rule in most companies is not about generosity toward employees, but "protect the boss, no matter the cost." And on the coattails of this precept of "save the king" comes "and save the hierarchy, too."

This unspoken rule frequently leads to outlandish protection for the biggest big shots and excessive protection for all who possess enough power to squeeze themselves into the fold of the elect. The outcome is that raw power is held by a small group of people who rationalize their value to the company and reward themselves accordingly, simply because they can. Even more insidious, it is usually done under the guise of protecting the company from the loss of the services of these "key players." These players, however, are often not key at all but simply people with the power to so define themselves.

13. Special privileges for the board

Originally, boards were set up to protect the shareholders. Today, in some cases, they have become the lackeys of the CEO; compensation committees are often stacked with friends of top management. In the other extreme, board members pose threats to the CEO's continued existence; ex-presidents and ex-chairmen get the bit in their teeth again and want to direct the show. Other times, essentially uninterested members contribute little or nothing, serving for the sake of the perks and because they like being on boards and having something to do.

I believe that in most cases, a responsible three-person board would be more effective than the twelve- and fifteen-member boards that are so often for show.

14. Abuses of travel policies

This one is simple: if the trip is not right and appropriate, do not take it. It is no more appropriate to use company funds to travel for free or because of boredom than it is to take corporate supplies for your children or lie on an expense account. Stealing is stealing. If I abuse my traveling privileges, and I have, I am stealing, not just from the company, but from myself.

15. Meetings in exotic locations

From the time I took charge at my company, I held meetings at the nicer corporate resort haunts from New York to Florida, on to Colorado, California, Hawaii, and places in between. I exposed people to new places and new things and used these meetings as a means of motivation for both management and the sales force. I gave awards and prizes and money, and I revved up employees and managers with speeches about how well we were doing and where the next great trip might be. I almost always included their wives and husbands and, at sales conventions, even let them substitute their mothers or grown children if they wished. I set no limit on their play activities and kept meeting times to a minimum. People were constantly excited about the trips and all the fun that came with them.

I did this again and again and again, and I did it in a consistently highly successful company, but in retrospect believe I was wrong. In the beginning, I did it more for me than for the managers and the employees, and later I did it because it had become a way of life. It was expensive and, while somewhat helpful, basically unnecessary. If I had to do it all over again, I would not do it at all. The organization, as successful as it was, would have been even stronger had I not.

16. Lengthy meetings

As far as I can see, a brief meeting will suffice in most cases, and a telephone conversation can usually accomplish the same thing as an in-person meeting.

If I felt a face-to-face meeting was necessary in my business, which was rare, my first thought was to have the other person come to me, from wherever in the country, instead of my going to him or her. I did enough required traveling to not want to add to this burden, and I always felt that making decisions from the decision-maker's seat was much more responsible than wasting time in airports, flying around, and being fed fancy meals I would not bother with at home.

It was, and remains, my thinking that any boss who is not simply a figurehead should have his rear in his seat and his ear to the phone. If you are the boss, you should be the most capable person around. Therefore, you should make the most decisions and all the important ones. This is hard to do when you cannot easily be reached.

Allowing a manager to remove him or herself from the day-to-day action is similar to the mistakes I watched people make with their sales forces. For years I watched as companies took the best salespeople out of their territories and made managers out of them. When it became my turn to decide, I left the best people in their territories, where they were productive, and made the management aspect of their jobs secondary. As usual, I found that properly paid and motivated salespeople can do just about anything they set their minds to. In this way, I did not lose a top producer's production. I paid him or her handsomely for the main job, as I had before, and then paid extra for every new task they shouldered. It was simple, which I always find preferable, and it worked.

I am also against meetings that go on and on for no reason other than to meet and say we met. The purpose of a meeting is to decide what to do; the result of reaching the decision should be to get up and get on with it, not keep talking about it. The guy who said, "Hold your meetings with the thermostat set at fifty-eight degrees and everyone standing up," may not have been my cousin, but he is surely my brother under the skin.

17. Corporate jets

Flying on a corporate jet is like floating around in your den, accompanied by a pleasantly mannered waitress whose function is to pamper you. No wonder so many take advantage of the experience. I believe, however, because it is so attractive, people tend to do so too often. In many cases, managers need reasons to stay at home and do their jobs, not incentives to take a recess from them. Should the top people in a big company have access to private jets at times? Absolutely. Just not the unlimited access that supposed "security scares" and "time delays" seem to justify today. The private plane is still the big prize of the game. Maybe it should be seen for what it is: a seductive convenience that fosters abuse and, therefore, needs careful monitoring.

18. Overwork

Obviously, if I got to the top on my own merit, there were times I worked hard along the way. When I was a young salesman, I would write proposals at home at night or on the weekends. Sometime later, I spent years playing racquetball at 6:30 in the morning so I could get to work by 8:00. In ensuing years, I even went to work at 6:00 a.m. for a while (and went home early) just to keep the people on the East Coast on their toes.

Despite this, I never worked harder than I needed to in order to accomplish my tasks, nor did I expect others to. I did not ask people to overwork, and if I saw them doing so, I sent them home to their families. I perceived it to be an issue of fairness.

These are just some of the things I view as ill-considered in business, each an example of the opportunities available for increased efficiency or cost reduction in an organization. These examples show that if you determine not to accept the status quo, improvement and added profit can come as easily from looking within the organization as it can from looking outside.

An Introduction to Sales

Is there more to business than what these broad brushstrokes suggested? Yes, of course, but not much more. What's left is mainly finite stuff, specific and definable problems that are not hard to get a handle on. As a former salesman, though, I must add some thoughts about that most important aspect of every business. Without continual progress in this area, unless you are a utility or have a monopoly, there *is* no business.

Let me begin with my own introduction to sales. When I was in about the sixth grade and tired of wearing used clothes from the clothing drives at church, the school announced a fundraising project. Whoever sold the most raffle entries would get a brand new jacket. I took one look at the jacket and thought, "I really want that." Every kid who wanted to enter had thirty days in which to compete. Well, every day after school for that month, I did my homework quickly and then went knocking on apartment doors, doing my best to cheerfully convince people to spend a quarter or two to support the school and, perhaps, get their name drawn to win a "wonderful" prize.

My quest turned out to be far from easy. The people I approached, uninvited, were poor, tired, often cranky, and basically unwilling to part with their hard-earned money, of which they had little extra. (I can remember my mother telling me later that in that same timeframe our family once had only one dollar to our name.) I was somewhat surprised to find that the many rejections I encountered didn't deter me in the slightest. In fact, in some ways, I began to relish the process as a challenge. I wanted that jacket, and I felt that if I was finding it a difficult proposition to sell, my competition likely was too. If I wasn't going to win, I made certain that it wasn't going to be for a lack of effort.

Then, I won. What came of the win wasn't just the jacket, though. Rather, it was the lesson in perseverance, the unwillingness to be deterred by rejection.

That helped me enormously a number of years later when I was promoted from junior to senior salesman and, as the newbie, was handed the worst territory in Manhattan (Forty-second to Forty-sixth streets, west of Fifth Avenue, before they cleaned up Times Square). Aside from a few decent buildings on Broadway and Sixth Avenue, which is what it was called before someone decided to rename it The Avenue of the Americas, my territory, which one of the company's more experienced salesmen had just failed in, was, to say the least, barren ground.

On my first day in it, I took a hard look and a deep breath, dug down inside myself, and started to knock on doors. I had carried groceries home for women when I was not much bigger than the bags, had sold sodas at bingo nights, had hustled tickets outside football games, had talked myself into a pin-setting job in a bowling alley when I was barely fourteen, had a full-time job when I was fifteen, and then had outproduced other junior salesmen to get this opportunity. And I had won that jacket in sixth grade. Who was to say I couldn't do this? And so this I did.

It was hard work, but that never bothered me when the carrot seemed attractive. My new quest took me into some pretty seedy places: Times Square was a zoo, Eighth Avenue was prostitution alley, Forty-sixth Street and Ninth Avenue was the edge of Hell's Kitchen, Tenth Avenue had mob-money-counting parlors and who knows what else. And then, in the back of a warehouse on Eleventh Avenue, where my predecessor had not ventured, I found my very best customer, a large printing company.

The territory wasn't much, but it was mine, and I made the most of it while it was. My success there led me to a far better territory in short order, and with the confidence I had gained from my first success as a senior salesman, I never looked back.

The experience was what the toughest cold-canvassing sales jobs are supposed to be: challenging and, if successful, rewarding.

If my family had not been poor enough for me to want that jacket so badly in sixth grade, and to prompt me to earn money in all those other ways throughout my childhood and adolescence, perhaps I would have lacked the fortitude to keep knocking away until I reached Eleventh Avenue. Again, who knows what is good and what is bad in life, since what we often perceive as harmful— including an impoverished childhood—often turns out to be helpful? Who *really* knows?

This experience helped me realize that, regardless of whether you've been told to the contrary, salespeople are made, not born. Does this mean that everyone can be a salesperson? No. It means that everyone who desires to can become one, just as everyone who desires to can learn to play the piano if he or she is willing to work at it. Are some people "naturals" at sales? Certainly, just as some people easily learn music or languages or math. Should this discourage those who find the learning more difficult? Not at all.

What must professional salespeople comprehend and manifest?

1. A naturalness with being who they are and in selling from that space.

2. A willingness to work in a dedicated and single-minded fashion until the mission has been accomplished.

3. An understanding that every customer willing to see a salesperson has a need, even if it is sometimes just for human companionship, and recognition that the person who is not a customer today may well be one tomorrow.

4. Patience, courtesy, conviction, and goal orientation.

5. An understanding and constant awareness that their own time is money.

6. Cheerfulness expressed through a mind not easily depressed by rudeness or rejection, and yet full acceptance of the fact that while the prospects have an inherent right to say no, salespeople have an inherent right to return and try again later.

7. An inclination to listen, coming from the understanding that all customers will tell the salesperson how to sell them if only he or she will be patient and let them do so. Professional salespeople tell the prospects all they know and then sell them whatever they wish to buy.

8. Proper grooming, attire, manners, and speech.

9. A better-than-average work ethic (required by all those who, in effect, work for themselves).

10. The ability to be silent the moment the prospect begins to speak.

11. Personal enjoyment from their own pitches, like an actor or actress presenting to an audience; here, however, the audience pays with its money's worth of time.

12. A preset determination to ask for the order at the right moment and a willingness, if that moment seems elusive, to ask what needs to be accomplished to bring it about. Good salespeople recognize there are many ways to ask for the business, and they use these methods over and over again.

13. The good sense to leave as soon as they get the order!

All in all, salespeople need internal motivation to handle often difficult assignments. Even more, they need a deep desire to make money and "win the contest," which is what sales is—initially—about, along with a significant willingness to expend the energy required to do so. Only those in whom such characteristics truly exist lie potentially successful salespeople.

Tea Cans, Managers, and Employees

As the components, and mistakes, of any business are easily defined, so too are the basics: Sell X per month, spend Y doing so, and Z (or minus Z) is the profit (or loss). Yes, you must account for all the variables, such as ensuring that future as well as present expenses are accounted for, that sufficient investments are made in research and development, and that no expense is overlooked, ignored, or underfunded. All of that, however, is never as complicated as it appears. The expense side of any company's books, now set up in a vast number of categories in a computer system, is no more complicated than my mother's tea cans.

Let me explain: When I was a child, my father, who was paid in cash, brought his pay home every week. My mother would divide up the cash, putting the appropriate amounts into different tea cans, which she had labeled "Gas and Electric," "Rent," "Food," and so on. When the gas and electric bill arrived, she would reach into the can and take out the money.

So despite all the fancy terms for accounts and subaccounts and the like, your company's sophisticated accounting system is really nothing more than a blown-up version of my father's income and my mother's tea cans. Once good managers understand this, the only real question they have left to ask about that part of the business is, "Do I have enough in each of the buckets to meet my future obligations?"

The deeper level of management is more difficult, but not much more complicated. It basically requires that you do the following:

- Reduce costs on a consistent basis.

- Train the employees to do a better job.

- Develop and maintain team spirit and pride in the company.

- Innovate without doing away with the fundamentals that brought the organization thus far.

- Pay respectful attention to, but do not be foolishly bullied by, the shareholders.

- Discard all mistaken programs and bad ideas as soon as they are recognized as such.

- Never forget that quality comes first.

- Do not seek short-term glory at the expense of long-term investment.

- Do whatever is necessary to keep properly priced, and I do mean "properly priced," sales flowing in and retained.

Fulfilling the requirements of these two levels of management (the first being primarily mechanical, the second motivational) would seem to guarantee the success of any business, but the real stability of an organization is achieved at a third, and often unseen, level. What makes a company resilient and durable is not a new product or team concept or downsizing or an inspired leader. Long-term survival and stability, both in good times and bad, is the result of consistent fairness to those who make up the organization. So, yes, companies need good leaders and decent products and new methods and innovative services and effective strategies. But what they need far more is the sustained development of a safe, caring environment in which their employees feel reasonably treated as they go about their daily tasks.

Executives and managers worthy of the name never forget one thing: *the employees are the company.*

4

The Challenges

When Being Right Is Wrong

Business can be, and should be, defined simply as problem-solving, part of a daily challenge. This is true not only from the viewpoint that encountering difficulties in business is inevitable, but also, and more importantly, from the perspective of whether you decide to deal with those challenges personally or impersonally. For it is this that will make you successful—or not. If you are willing to look upon problems anew, you can see that they are the nutrients of growth. Like mistakes, problems are literally your teachers. Once you accept this, you will also see, no matter your initial reactions, that the reasonable response to their arisal is not, "Why does this always happen to me?" but "What should I do about this?"

As a trained firefighter puts out fires, a competent businessperson solves problems. Problems of any nature or size, like fires of any nature or size, call for immediate action, your function being to undo them completely, extinguishing them as carefully as you would a campfire, lest it well up and develop the strength to turn your peaceful forest into an ugly conflagration.

With this in mind, a reasonable grading system in any organization would go something like this:

- A poor employee is careless, causing problems instead of solving them.
- A decent employee solves problems after they occur.
- A good employee solves problems as they are happening.
- An outstanding employee solves problems before they take place.

Sometimes being proactive about problems will lead you into uncharted waters, even so far as to needing to violate certain protocol or rules. If you wish to be a better-than-average employee or manager, however, you cannot let fear of reprisal prevent you from taking unusual action when you are certain it is warranted. The idea is to follow the course that seems to make the most sense for the good of the company.

At the same time, there is always wisdom to be found in soliciting other opinions and, when the issue is serious, trying to find a partner in the matter, preferably your boss. Yet when it comes to crunch time, that is, when a situation calls for immediate action, you must do what feels right. If that results in your being fired, so be it. If you are your own person, you will leave with your head held high.

Something similar once happened to me. After I left New York for a sales manager's job in Northern California, I had a quick succession of experiences. Still with Friden, I built the sales force up quickly and successfully, and thanks to that and the help of the good fellow I was working for, in about nine months I was promoted to a small branch manager's position in Southern California. Six months or so later, I was offered a much larger branch in Connecticut and took it.

No sooner was I in Connecticut than I was recruited by some ex-Friden people to become the New York branch manager for

Dura Business Machines. The offer had the potential for a large increase in income, and since this was about the time that I had lost a lot of money in the market, I accepted after refusing a counter-offer from Friden, with the proviso that Dura would repay Friden for my relocation. I was back to commuting an hour and a half into the city, but the new company had a great location on Madison Avenue, an attractive product line, untapped territories, and a management group in California that trusted me and left me alone to do what I needed to do.

We were almost instantly successful. There were more than a few good people already in the company, most of whom needed no more than some direction and better incentives. In addition, people who knew me or had worked for me at Friden were easily recruited. I started making far more money than I had ever made before. The company set no limits on my income, splitting the profits of the branch with me fifty-fifty. With the blessings of management, I also put together a used-machine sales and service company of my own. In addition to my growing monthly income, leasing companies, forms companies, data-processing services companies, and the like each paid and entertained us in order to capture the spinoff results of our sales.

It was as though I had become the main character in a good movie, my luck abounding in Hollywood proportions. I moved back to the last town I had lived in, in New Jersey, buying a nice house near some friends who still lived there. Our sales, which were low when I arrived, grew almost immediately and, after a while, astronomically. In less than a year, I was promoted to eastern division manager. I recruited other people I knew to become branch managers, and they quickly became successful, adding to my reputation and income. The chairman of the company was so pleased with my performance that he stopped by to hand me the keys to a luxury car as a gift. I was back in the heart of "action city." I was young, I was afloat in cash, and I was living the high life: succeeding, being well-compensated, partying, and having a great time.

Then Dura was sold to Itel Corporation, a mini-conglomerate set up by an entrepreneurial type and a few ex-executives from IBM. We got off to a fine beginning; they left my income structure intact and added a few branches to my domain. They flattered me, entertained me at exotic locations, and treated me well in every possible way. This, obviously, was not because they loved me, but because they felt they needed me, the reasons for which soon became evident, together with their reasons for buying the company.

The first move they decided on in their very limited wisdom (they really didn't know this portion of the industry or the company and hadn't asked anyone's opinion other than their own) was to double the size of the sales force. Now, at times, increasing the size of a sales force, if carefully managed, can be a helpful step in the direction of increased sales. What these fellows did not realize, however, was that although we were a business-equipment company, we were not IBM. We were instead a company grown, nurtured, and maintained by fiercely independent, hard-nosed, cold-calling, and quite capable straight-commission salespeople whose territories were sacrosanct to them; you touched the size of it only at the real risk of losing the salesperson to a competitor. Plus, unbeknownst to the new owners, because they had done a poor job of due diligence, the equipment we sold, while as attractive as business equipment could be, had one major flaw: it kept breaking down.

As soon as I became aware of their plans, I scheduled a meeting with them at which I informed them that I believed they were about to make a major mistake. I suggested that instead of going forward, we devote the following six to twelve months to eliminating the design flaws that were causing the almost constant equipment failures, and that during this time we make plans to gradually increase the size of the sales force. They were respectful and said they would consider my arguments, but I left unconvinced that they meant what they said. And when they called a few days later to say that they were going forward with their own plan, I was not surprised.

I was, though, disturbed. I was still young and inexperienced enough to take what happens in business personally, and I was ticked off because I saw them tampering with the goose that was laying my golden eggs. What I should have done, since I had already done my best to give them the facts as I saw them, was to say, "Yes, sir," and quietly begin to look for another job. I should also have not ignored my mother's advice to me when I was younger, which was "If you don't have to put it in writing, don't."

So I sat down and crafted a well-reasoned, yet essentially quixotic missive, designed to change their minds, save the structure until the foundation could be strengthened, and ultimately preserve the income from my cushy job. What I didn't understand at the time was that this was a company bent on quick action, with a strategy of buying companies to pump them up and then dispose of them, not one based on solving problems and staying around for the long run. To boot, it was a public company, which meant that as soon as they read about the previously undiscovered, or at least undiscussed, issues that I had now put into writing, they really had only two choices: agree with me and postpone their plans or let me go.

They chose the latter. They fired me not, obviously, for performance, but for, and in this sense perhaps rightly so, the unwise youthful exuberance and selfishness that I exhibited, which didn't end up assisting anyone. Should they have listened to me? Yes. Nine months or so after I left, they discharged the company's president, an ex-IBM powerhouse and one of their own. A year after that, they closed down the entire organization in order to quell a torrent of red ink. Nonetheless, should I have paid attention to my mother? Yes. My unsolicited and unhelpful letter served no useful purpose. And while I was right and I left unashamed, because I took the matter beyond the boundaries of good sense, I was also wrong.

Everyone Counts

What else is there in the challenge of running a business? Not much. In part, as mentioned, it is like making the orchestra work well, but the other part is more like tending to a somewhat off-balance machine that needs preventive maintenance and constant care than anything else.

One thing more to see, though, again from that third level of management, is how effective leaders care enough about their employees to raise them to their limits, while remaining careful not to push them beyond. These are the leaders who are truly helpful, wise enough to overlook the problems with authority of those beneath them, while putting limits on their expression so it does not harm the work. Good leaders seek to defuse the obnoxious, work patiently with the malcontent, and recognize always that their function is impersonal.

Potentially solid performers with great latent talent hide in every organization, disguised by their defensiveness and discontent. It is the boss's responsibility to aid in removing these obstructions, seeking out those who are ripe to leave the womb of youthful rebellion and emerge into a more mature way of reacting to the challenges of work. In any solid organization, where everyone is understood as a potential contributor, everyone counts. Thus, learning to be sensitive to the emotional needs of the company's employees is an important business practice, even in the mildest of cases. If I come to work in the morning and say, "Hi, Sally, how are you today?" and she responds with some version of, "Oh, okay," rather than her usual cheerful greeting, it is up to me to realize Sally is in distress and might benefit from a moment of my consideration.

This approach to management is much more difficult than managing by the rules. It requires attention, sensitivity, and a commitment to everyone in the organization. It recognizes that the employees' attitudes reflect on their work, and that improving the quality of their work is part of a manager's work.

In an effective work environment, real common sense, which is the reflection of wisdom, always sets the course for the betterment of everyone, which must include respect for everyone. Without respect, businesspeople are inevitably caught in the confusion of self-centeredness, along with its fear of failure and success alike.

The Good News and the Bad News

On your way to becoming a more effective business leader, respect of others begins with finding reason to respect yourself. One of the best ways to build stronger character is to accept the idea that you are capable of finding a way around every hindrance to your advancement. Let us, for example, consider some of the common problems that you may perceive, which I mentioned earlier in passing, and explore some fast, simple, and practical responses to what may be the mind's bitterness and complaints.

Common Problems and Practical Responses to the Mind's Resistance

1. Business is a man's game.
   Learn to play it.

2. Your best friend does not always understand you.
   Understand him when he is temporarily incapable of understanding you.

3. Your mother is not always kind.
   These are the times when she most needs your kindness.

4. Minorities are sometimes discriminated against.
   If you are in the majority, never discriminate. If you are a minority, learn to walk through all inclinations toward self-pity.

5. Some days you feel horrible.
   Try to get a good night's sleep in anticipation of a better tomorrow, and avoid making it more complicated than that.

6. The most qualified person does not always get the job.
   There are jobs yet to come and lessons to be learned that
   are much more important than any one particular job.

7. Your body does not always function perfectly.
   Accept that and, to the degree possible, shape it up.

8. Your boss is not unfailingly appreciative.
   Neither are you.

9. A number of people in the world are more intelligent than
   you are.
   Many successful, happy, and fulfilled people in the world
   are less intelligent than you are.

10. You may not end up with an inheritance.
    If it leads you to self-reliance, it could be a more valuable
    gift.

11. There are those who dislike you without cause.
    Accept yourself while changing what you do not like
    about yourself, and refuse all inclinations to dislike others
    in return.

12. The world is not always fair.
    That is its challenge.

As Epictetus (the freed Roman slave and stoic philosopher, ca. 100 CE) taught, and as Kenneth Wapnick continues to teach, you cannot change the world, but you can change the influence you let it have on you. The way to escape from the seemingly external reboundings of what are in actuality your own projections of negativity is to understand that what you experience with people and events comes not from them, but from your interpretations and therefore from you. It is the bias of misunderstood past experiences, and the distorted memories and beliefs that resulted from them, that produce the platform from which we so often misperceive. Present intelligence will disclose this to you when you are ready to accept it. With this awareness you will see that the main thing you can glean from your confused past, and all its muddled musings, is the honesty that comes with the recognition of how often you were mistaken in what you thought was true. This insight should assist you in remembering to question the "learning" these misperceptions produced, and not to rely solely on them as the light to guide you now.

Another thing to understand as you gain a more sensible outlook on life is that no matter how difficult your past experiences, if you like where you are right now, those experiences were part of how you got here; therefore, you should be thankful for them and to everyone involved. This is the way to awaken from the corrupting graveyard of blame and regret to the freshness of a life lived fully and without resentment.

What this leads to as well is the recognition that no one is going to come along and hand you the keys to wisdom on a silver platter. True wisdom is neither an accumulation of information, nor a time-oriented concept; rather, it is a state you discover within yourself after traveling through the fog of your negative memories, with all their pain, prejudices, and ignorance.

So, in the simplest of terms, there is good news and bad news. The bad news is that no one is going to show up and rescue you. The good news is that you are quite capable of rescuing yourself. This means that instead of pleading for the answer, you should become the answer, recognizing at last that *the leader you are searching for is you.*

PART II

SUCCESS

5

"The More"

Childish Whims

What is success? The dictionary defines it as a favorable outcome and, more specifically, as "the attainment of wealth, favor or eminence."[15] I find these definitions incomplete and, for our purposes, wrong. Every "outcome" is incidental; sometimes you win, sometimes you lose, sometimes the golf shot goes straight, sometimes not. Therefore, can what is unpredictable and not really up to you be deemed favorable or unfavorable? It cannot. To people lost in the thrall of business, however, success has nothing to do with a peaceful acceptance of life as it presents itself, only with winning and thereby gaining "the more."

The great fable of "the more" goes something like this: the more you get your hands on, the more you will have. Unfortunately, though, what happens is that the more you have, the more you believe you deserve, and the more you believe you deserve, the more you want. More of this and more of that. Once caught up in the hypnosis of competing for more, you will never be satisfied with what you currently have. This is how it was for me in my earlier days.

When I was a young salesman in Manhattan, I happened to be in the office one day when our previous sales manager, now a branch manager in New Jersey, stopped by for a visit with our branch manager. Seated near them, I could not help overhearing their conversation, which was about our visitor's recent trip to Pebble Beach with some colleagues and all the fun they had. At the time, I had played golf less than a dozen times and knew nothing about good golf courses, much less Pebble Beach. But the guy was a personable, attractive character, their conversation and laughter were stimulating, and the specialness of such a trip seemed exciting to me. What happened next? I quickly formulated a long-term goal. I made the determination that I, too, would one day be among those invited to go to that special place, Pebble Beach, and that I, like this guy, would come back to the office to meet with others and talk about all the fun.

As time went on and I grew in my career, I was invited to go with the group to play golf at Pebble Beach. And then later, I was the one doing the inviting. Later still, I was holding meetings there, and that same personable fellow and others like him were working for me. I'm sorry to be the second one to tell you there is no Santa Claus, but do you know what playing Pebble (and Spyglass and Cypress Point), staying in the best suites in The Lodge, and soaking in the specialness of it all did for me? Beyond leaving me with the ability to spout forth that I had done so, it did nothing but fulfill a childish whim.

There is nothing wrong with what I accomplished. There is always value in making up your mind to do something and then going out and doing it. The accomplishment can teach you that you are more capable than you may have believed and that what excites you is not what it appears to be. In that sense, much was positive in what I accomplished. Yet did it make me a better person or bring me contentment? Not at all.

And that is the real point in life: working to undo your faults and, in that, becoming a better person. So if I seek happiness, I must use the means that lead to that end. Every positive goal requires the use of similar means. Therefore, the misuse of means, even when leading to a particular end, always results in failure. Let me give you an example of my youthful confusion about this, in this case trying to help one person at the expense of another.

One night, when I was in my mid-twenties, my closest buddy and I were in the bar he owned at closing time without the money between us to meet his rent payment, which was due the following morning. This was going to cost him the bar. Then along came a guy who, strangely enough for our neighborhood, had just received an inheritance. I had the "bright" idea of hustling him at dice to get the rent payment, which we then proceeded to do. Success! We saved the bar and my friend's business.

That little trick haunted me for years. Was it an acceptable action because this was my best friend, and the loss of his business was imminent? Of course not. Did we even pause to think about just asking the guy for a loan and taking the chance he might say no? Of course not. We had the single-minded goal of saving the bar, and we were not going to be told no. Did the end justify the means? Was saving one person's business a possible justification for cheating another? Of course not. Would it have been acceptable that my friend actually lost his business? If he found his virtue in the process, yes.

The point here, which unfortunately took me a long time to learn, is that there is no free lunch. Not only are the improper schemes you are often suggested to chase after laced with shards of disappointment, but also, even when denied, with the lingering aftertaste of self-loathing. When anyone with above-average talent or wit, be he a gambler, politician, prosecutor, fighter, businessman, financial expert, or the like, abuses those qualities, taking advantage of the less fit, he is unknowingly proclaiming that his desires have greater value than his virtue. And underneath all of his smug satisfaction about getting his way, that person will find only regret for the loss of his awareness of that virtue, that loss being the incredible cost of his supposed gain.

No matter how successful the con, how attractive the dressing, how exciting the seeming victory, be it cheating at dice or cards, overpowering another, abusing insider information, not paying your fair share of the common tax burden, even leaving work undone for someone else to do, actions taken at the expense of others always wound the one who acts in such ways.

Nothing and Everything

Ideas too readily accepted, especially in the heat of excitement, often develop into concepts about what is valuable. As time goes on, those false concepts combine to form part of the thought system from which you desire, decide, and act. In many cases it is this self-developed and distorted belief system that "helps" you to determine your goals, telling you what is worth striving for now, based on what you, in your confusion and youthful exuberance, told it was important before.

My first truly fancy home was an excellent example of this. It was an all-glass contemporary perched over the fourth green of an exclusive country club, with sparkling views of lush fairways and of the ocean beyond. When I was younger, I had been in a number of fancy homes and always admired them; they were a symbol of what I then perceived as one of the greatest proofs of "arrival." However, when I arrived and purchased my own symbol, I found nothing but intrusion. There was always the bother of a non-family member in or around the house: a daily maid, three weekly gardeners, a pest-control man, tree men to keep the trees and shrubbery under control, a pool man to take care of the fountain and waterfall, electricians to maintain the outside lighting and speakers. And that's not to mention the marble specialists, painters, and sundry repairmen, decorators, and window washers. Experts in this or that always seemed to be around. Did the place look great? Yes. Did visitors usually say, "What a lovely house!"? Yes. Did it offer me contentment, security, privacy, and quiet? Not at all.

That "the more" is actually more is one of the great deceptions of the mind. But "the more" no longer works for me; neither, I believe, does it really work for others.

Not that many years ago, I had lunch with a no-longer-young ex-vice presidential candidate. He was a national figure. Obviously, he had lost, however, and was now out of politics and into business. He did not seem much interested in national or international subjects any more. In fact, all he could talk about was his exciting new business venture and how he just knew it would succeed. Think about it: Get through a tough life, full of bruising battles. Become a powerful politician, well-known on the national stage. Thereafter, have an instantly recognizable face, as well as an international reputation. Reach a ripe old age and find yourself mainly interested in one more business deal—to reach more of "the more." To him, sensible. To me, questionable.

I used to play golf with a (now deceased) multi-multi-millionaire who after missing a shot often threw his club farther than he had hit his ball, cursing loudly as he did so. Was he truly successful? Clearly not. I had a father who did custodial work impeccably and with a *dignitas* unmatched in most corporate boardrooms. Was he successful? Absolutely.

Helping my father at work as a boy (before my rebellion kicked in) helped me learn later that the "what" of life is nothing more than the particular position you occupy at this moment. The "how" is your performance within that role. *What* is nothing; *how* is everything. The world states with certitude that title, position, and influence all have great meaning, yet in truth they are neutral: means, not ends. To be the best (banker, lawyer, father, mother, gravedigger, nurse) you can be at this moment, in this situation, is to fill a neutral form with content, to find the end you seek right here and right now.

This does not mean that you always do what you do perfectly. Neither does it suggest that you spend countless hours at it, or do not spend countless hours at it. Perhaps it is your present love. All it means is that you do your very best with what you have now.

If you seek a high-profile wealth-larded life and place that goal before personal growth, you will get exactly what you seek, which means you lose even when you seem to gain. Like many, you may believe that to walk the aisles of any store able to purchase anything you see means freedom. Real freedom, however, is walking those aisles and not being taken in by the glitter of what you see. This doesn't mean that you don't buy things; it just means you no longer believe you cannot do without them. In effect, you sometimes like, but you no longer lust.

Yet, to one still lost in the madness of consumption and the accumulation of the more, even the $475,000 watch recently featured in *The Robb Report* makes some kind of sense. It is only when you come to accept yourself as a student that you can see your Rolex as just a timepiece; your suit, no matter how fine its cloth and cut, only a uniform; your car merely a means of transportation; excessive servants a bother; the jet a convenience; and the house, or houses, no matter the number of rooms or grandeur of the grounds, no more than a roof over your head when you go to sleep.

A buccaneer of business rarely perceives his golden bracelets as handcuffs and his house as just another tent in the big-tent competition. How could he? For if he understood their essential neutrality and basic meaninglessness, then what he did to get them would cease to have meaning as well. Yet what would he do if he stopped striving for the more? Who would he be if he did not run and fight and win and outgain? Unable to face the thought that his existence so far has been senseless, he fears the loss of wanting as though it were a loss of self. Yet, as intimidating as that may sound, he must ask himself whether the more is actually more or whether it is merely like an appetite that grows as it is fed.

Look around you. There has to be something askew with the whole system when you see a seventy-five-year-old multi-multi-millionaire jumping up and down in excitement because his horse just won a race. He did not win the race; his horse did. All he did was pay for it. Someone else trained the horse, another person rode the horse, and the horse itself ran the race. So why is he so overjoyed? Did the horse's victory make him a winner? Surely he is behaving as though it had. Would he be as equally deprived and depressed if the horse had lost the race? If so, why? It is only a horse race, after all, and at that, just one race among many.

Disunity and Isolation

Some 125 years ago, Fyodor Dostoevsky wrote the following in *The Brothers Karamazov* about such men with such needs:

> The world has proclaimed freedom, especially of late, but what do we see in this freedom of theirs, only "slavery and suicide." For the world says: "You have needs, therefore satisfy them, for you have the same rights as the noblest and richest men. Do not be afraid to satisfy them, but even increase them"—this is the current teaching of the world. And in this they see freedom. But what comes of this right to increase one's needs? For the rich, *isolation* … for the poor, envy and murder, for they have been given rights, but have not yet been shown any way of satisfying their needs…. Taking freedom to mean the increase and prompt satisfaction of needs, they distort their own nature, for they generate many meaningless and foolish desires, habits, and the most absurd fancies in themselves….
>
> And no wonder that instead of freedom they have fallen into slavery, and instead of serving brotherly love and human unity, they have fallen, on the contrary, into disunity and isolation…. They have succeeded in amassing more and more things, but have less and less joy.[16]

Have things really improved since then?

6

The Specter of Failure

An Incessant Hunger

Winning and losing are two sides of the same coin, both inventions of limited imaginations. In business, they are called success and failure, each gaining meaning from its contrast with the other. The greater the belief in the contrast, the more frantically you run from one and toward the other, chasing desperately after what you think is important. For example, if you believe success means promotions, then remaining in the same job, even with good raises, becomes failure to you. If traveling means you "have arrived," then staying at home represents your shortfall. If you believe you lack the more, even if you have enough, you will always see yourself as incomplete and, in that, your success as a failure.

In *American Mania—When More Is Not Enough*, Dr. Whybrow writes that "Americans are addictively driven by the brain's pleasure centers to live turbocharged lives in pursuit of status and possessions." Of businesspeople, he says, "They don't need that extra money but they want that extra money and are moving too fast for [their own] good."[17]

Albert Einstein once said, "Even when I was a fairly precocious young man, the nothingness of the hopes and stirrings which chase most men restlessly through life came to my consciousness with considerable vitality. Moreover, I soon discovered the cruelty of that chase which was carefully covered up by hypocrisy and glittering words."[18]

Consider the following suggestion from Epictetus about avoiding the chase altogether:

> Remember that in life you ought to behave as at a banquet. Suppose that something is carried round and is opposite to you. Stretch out a hand and take a portion with decency. Suppose it passes you by. Do not detain it. Suppose that it is not yet come to you. Do not send your desire forward to it, but wait till it is opposite you. Do so and you will become a worthy partner of the banquets.[19]

Now this from Plato's *Laws*:

> Athenian: [It is] the passion for wealth which leaves a man not a moment of leisure to attend to anything beyond his personal fortunes. So long as a citizen's whole soul is wrapped up in these, he cannot give a thought to anything but the day's takings. Any study or pursuit which tends to that result, everyone sets himself eagerly to learn and practice. All others are laughed to scorn.
>
> Clinias: Too true.
>
> Athenian: Well then, this, as I say, may be set down for one reason which tends to keep societies from efficient cultivation of nobler activities.... It turns the naturally quiet and decent man into a ... mere menial and makes the more adventurous ... swashbucklers and bullies, though often enough they are not so much vicious as unfortunate.
>
> Clinias: Unfortunate? Why so?

Athenian: Why, what epithet but "most unfortunate" can I find for men who are forced to go through the world with an incessant hunger gnawing at their souls?[20]

The Right Place

All of these examples speak of the usual lot of the "me first," material-success-only-oriented businesspeople, especially the more competent among them, who believe it foolish to abandon an arena, no matter its disappointments, where the advantage is so clearly theirs. Here they abide, living a life in which spates of elation are always followed by bouts of frustration and foreboding, often successful but rarely content. To them, success in worldly affairs is a sure sign of favor from the deities; failure, therefore, is interpreted as unfair or a punishment.

This makes no sense once you realize that if you invest in outcomes, you are setting yourself up for future indignation over what you will end up considering to be life's failures in relationship to you. The fact is that fate and fortune have their own rules: things do not always turn out the way you hope, you do not always get what you want, and people do not always do as you wish. Yet really, so what? These outcomes only seem unfavorable when you forget that your purpose is to succeed in this, the constant act of learning from everything, be that thing called good or bad by others.

So how can you avoid forgetting to remember to learn from everything? By staying with each issue you encounter until you finally recognize that they all have the same answer because they are all the same: the issue is *never* about others; it is *always* about you. Let me give you a simple example of something I came to learn about my thinking when I was young.

When I was about nine or so, my father would sometimes borrow the pastor's car on a Sunday afternoon to take the family for a drive. Preferring to play ball with my friends, a family drive was never something I wanted to do, but it wasn't open to choice, so I went. At times we went to visit relatives, but more often to visit various friends of my parents; so it was sometimes okay, sometimes boring. There was, however, one place we visited occasionally that, for reasons I could not understand, really bothered me.

Not far from where we had lived in Yonkers, near the car dealership my father had worked in as a mechanic, lived a family whom my parents were close to. The father was the sales manager of the dealership, in some part due to my father, through whose influence he got his first job there as a salesman. This was a position my father was unable to secure for himself, despite the fact he had the personality for it, because he had left school after the third grade and didn't, therefore, have the skills it required.

The people were as pleasant as could be. They lived in a nice house on a quiet tree-lined street, had two particularly nice children, including a boy near my age, and were always glad to see us. Furthermore, they were seemingly quite grateful to my father. Yet every time we went there I found myself disturbed, disliking the man and, in some ways, the boy, which made no sense to me even then. After all, they could not have been kinder to us.

Years later, when I did my own, shall we say, personal inventory, I thought more deeply about this issue, which was still lingering about because I had not resolved it. I discovered why I was disturbed with the man and the boy, and realized that I was also actually bothered by my father and, as always, underneath all that, myself. The reason: I was secretly accusing my father of failure and these people of living my life.

In my childish notions of who should get what in the world and who should not, I was condemning my father for not stepping up to the plate and figuring out how to be courageous enough to get the sales job. Why? Because had he done so, he would have that sales manager's position, which would put me, not in that small apartment amid the aggressiveness of the Bronx, but rather in that nice house on the quiet, tree-lined street where these people who, in my immature thinking, had taken my place now lived instead of me.

By the time I got to look at this lingering dislike, examine its causes, and let it perish, I was old enough to realize the following:

1. *These people had given me no reason to dislike them.* Even if they had, it wouldn't have changed the fact that I was the sole cause of how I felt about them.

2. *It was not my father's fault he left school early; he was forced to go to work.* In addition, if he was too afraid, too insecure, or more likely, too weary in later life to add the education required to secure a better-paid position, who was I, in my youthful determinations, to accuse him, a good, hardworking man, of malfeasance for not doing so?

3. *In reality, my reactions had nothing to do with this family or my father's supposed inadequacies.* Rather, my reactions had everything to do with my own inadequacies, along with my confused belief that if only I lived on that street and in that house, I would be as happy as I imagined that boy to be.

4. *The Bronx had been the perfect place for me to learn how to deal with an often harsh world.* All of the aggression and abuse I encountered and survived there was helpful in many ways. Therefore, living in that nice house on the quiet street may well have been far less helpful, at least for a person like me.

5. *I could use this one example to uncover the incorrectness of my beliefs in many other situations.* Most, if not all, of those incorrect beliefs related to something I will talk more about later: the common error of blaming others, usually starting with our parents, for the discomfort we feel or the mistakes we make. My oldest son, who died, was a good

example of this. One day, he said to me in his distress, "It's not my fault I'm in this state. You're the one who brought me here," (meaning into the world).

6. *Understanding the mind's tendency to leapfrog over the positive and land on the negative can help you recognize that you are not only in the right place, but have also always been in the right place.* I can remember a time when my son—the same boy who died—was having serious difficulty with his life. During that period, the star athlete son of a fellow who worked for me landed on the cover of a national sports magazine. My mind's first inclination was to draw an unfavorable comparison between my situation and his, and to believe, again, that I was being cheated by life, in juxtaposition to receiving fatherly glory, as this other fellow was. Being older and wiser by then, however, I had reached a stage of being grateful to my children for how much they had taught me about looking at them with appreciation, even in the midst of their sometimes terrible struggles. This mindset allowed me to quickly remember how fortunate I was to have such a son, who was, despite his painful way of living, a very nice person, and how too, just like the Bronx had been where I belonged back then, being this boy's father and not the other's was the right position for me now.

The Harder Road

As with most important things, the truth of what life is about—that there is no good or bad, only the constant act of learning—must be approached with care. In his book *The Pleasure of Finding Things Out*, the physicist Richard Feynman speaks to the need for honesty in observing and reporting objectively. He says: "I believe that in the judgment of evidence, the reporting of evidence and so on, there is a kind of responsibility which the scientists feel toward each other which you can represent as a kind of morality. What's the right way and the wrong way to report results? Disinterestedly, so that the other man is free to understand precisely what you are saying, and as nearly as possible not covering it over with your desires…. This … helps each of us to understand each other."[21] If we are to grow in a healthy fashion, I believe this kind of objectivity should extend to the way we observe and "report on" our thinking, since honesty is the only real way to learn about ourselves.

To see the wisdom in looking with skepticism on your good opinions, as well as on the bad ones, is to begin to free yourself from the too-often false resoluteness of belief itself. Walt Whitman's outlook on this was quite clear. He said, "Re-examine all you have been told at school or church or in any book. Dismiss what insults your own soul."[22]

This idea about belief may be elemental, but it is not necessarily apparent: It is belief that influences how you think, and in turn, how you see and react to the world. Once you understand this, you will likely realize that you have often allowed prejudice to pose as sense and worry to pose as reasoning and that all these dark and foolish fancies must be exposed for the frauds they are. Because without their interference the mind is naturally efficient, capable of resolving what is essentially the mundane in issue after issue, having no more of a personal feeling about any of them than has the clerk behind the counter calling to a subsequent customer, "Next!"

Epictetus understood what was important, as the following story about him demonstrates:

> When a certain person came to him, who was going up to Rome on account of a suit which had regard to his rank, Epictetus inquired the reason of his going to Rome, and the man then asked what he thought about the matter. Epictetus replied: If you ask me what you will do in Rome, whether you will succeed or fail, I have no rule about this. But if you ask me how you

will fare, I can tell you: if you have right opinions you will fare well; if they are false you will fare ill. For to every man the cause of his acting is opinion. For what is the reason you desire to be elected governor of the Cnossians? Your opinion. What is the reason you are now going up to Rome? Your opinion. And going in winter, and with danger and expense? I must go [you say]. What tells you this? Your opinion. Then if opinions are the causes of all actions, and a man has bad opinions, such as the cause may be, such also is the effect. Have we then all sound opinions, both you and your adversary? And how do you differ? But have you sounder opinions than your adversary? Why? You think so. And so does he think that his opinions are better, and so do madmen. This is a bad criterion. But show to me that you have made some inquiry into your opinions, and have taken some pains about them. And as now you are sailing to Rome in order to become governor of the Cnossians, and you are not content to stay at home with the honors which you have, but you desire something greater and more conspicuous, so when did you ever make a voyage for the purpose of examining your own opinions, and casting them out, if you have any that are bad? Whom have you approached for this purpose? What time have you fixed for it? What age?[23]

In other words, real progress does not come from achieving "honors," but from self-examination. This means, as Epictetus told the traveler to Rome, you should re-examine all of your opinions. This does not suggest you do without teachers. Rather it states you are here to learn so well from everyone that you one day arrive at the recognition that the real teacher and student are within and are one. What you learn truly comes only through your agreement with the teaching, and that agreement—or lack thereof—comes from your freedom to choose to agree or disagree with anyone. This is your journey, as another's is his, and on it you must stand alone and decide for yourself.

This you will find is a difficult assignment, one that you will surely, at times, want to set aside for the sweet old ways of the good old days. Whenever you find yourself at one of these junctures, try to keep in mind how often those sweet old days turned bitter and sour, as well as the dissatisfaction that started you on the journey of self-inquiry to begin with. As you take this, the harder road, also remember that your deepest responsibility lies in your solemn promise never to give up and never to give in—above all, right after you have just given up and have just given in.

The idea is that the moment you catch a rational breath in what you may have been defining up to that point as your failure, cease beating yourself up over your lapse in attention and rob regret of its energy through doing nothing other than starting again. Your purpose, like everyone else's, includes being kind to yourself and excludes being pushed about by your thoughts and emotions. As you get better at setting their meaningless demands and persuasions aside, it will become apparent there is no such thing as permanent failure. In the acquisition of this longer-term view, it will also become clear that excitement and depression are just vacillations of the superficial mind.

The *I Ching,* the source of much of Confucianist and Taoist philosophy, offers the following advice about how to approach both extremes:

> When a man is advancing farther and farther, it is important for him not to become intoxicated by success. Precisely when he experiences great success, it is necessary to remain sober and not try to skip any stages; he must go on slowly, step by step, as though hesitant. Only such calm, steady progress, overleaping nothing, leads to the goal.
>
> [There are also times when] an adverse fate [occurs] in human life. In such times, there is nothing a man can

do but acquiesce in his fate and remain true to himself. This concerns the deepest stratum of his being, for this alone is superior to all external fate.

When adversity befalls a man, it is important above all things for him to be strong and overcome the trouble inwardly. If he is weak the trouble overwhelms him. Instead of proceeding on his way, he falls ever more deeply into gloom and melancholy. This makes the situation only more and more hopeless. Such an attitude comes from an inner delusion that he must by all means overcome.[24]

In the piece "Rugby Chapel," the English poet Matthew Arnold wrote:

Most men eddy about
Here and there—eat and drink,
Chatter and love and hate,
Gather and squander, are raised
Aloft, are hurl'd into the dust
Striving blindly, achieving
Nothing; and then they die—[25]

Thoreau probably had the same viewpoint of humanity when he wrote, "The mass of men lead lives of quiet desperation."[26]

Both statements suggest that spending all of your time chasing after external rewards will not lift you out of the eddy of nothingness and desperation that you likely experience, as do most humans. That's not to say that to become free of the ordinary and its suffocating aims, you must abandon your job, go to the woods, and take up a life of fasting and prayer—because that of its own accord will not nurture the seeds of learning nor improve the state of your mental health. Only re-examining "all you have been told" and dismissing "what insults your own soul" can possibly accomplish that.

7

Perspective

The Value of "Uh-huh"

In the midst of the ambitious race after "success," which seems only to frighten us with its supposition of the reality of "failure," how do you find your bearings? One way is by learning to stand back from the mind's turmoil and angst. Let me give you a couple of examples of what I mean.

I don't take golf seriously now, but that wasn't always the case. I was never all that great at the game. My lowest handicap was eleven, but for a number of years I played to a fourteen, which is fairly average. I had my occasional moments of glory, though: a hole in one in my first year of playing and two more later, breaking eighty a few times, once shooting even par on the front side of Pebble Beach (I shot forty-seven on the back), and so on. These little seeming victories, however, in an immature mind filled with the desire to be special, often led me into believing that the golf gods should always bless my outings. This, in turn, frequently deceived me into forgetting that the point of golf was not to shoot a low score but to enjoy the day, a simple, but for me at times, hard to remember fact.

Watching my mind, however, even back then, before I knew I was supposed to, aided me enormously in getting past this forgetfulness. For instance, once while playing Spyglass, my all-time favorite golf course, I approached the sixth hole in a very disturbed state of mind. I don't remember now how I had played the first five holes, but whether it was well and I was fierce in my desire to continue playing that way, or it was poorly and I was angry about it, I was out of balance. I proceeded by hitting a bad drive on the sixth hole; I can still see myself pounding the club into the ground in frustration.

As I played number six, an uphill par four, and seven, a level par five, my mind continued to race around in a childish tantrum of seriousness and upset. But then as I approached the green on seven, which is bordered by a small pond, I looked at the stillness of the water and thought, "That is the way my mind is supposed to be, not disturbed like it is over what is really nothing."

Not long after that incident, the same thing happened at Mauna Kea, another great Robert Trent Jones course, on the Big Island of Hawaii. I was in a lovely place, playing a beautiful course in great weather and pleasant company, but because I was playing poorly, I wasn't enjoying any of it. On an uphill par four, I hit another in a series of bad shots, and as my mind started to jump up and down again, I had another quiet thought, this one saying: "This is not right; the reasonable way to look on something like this is in peace and equanimity." I didn't realize it at the time, but the "something like this" meant not only the shot, but also all my thinking about how unfair such circumstances were to this self-important character called me.

Each time I had a similar challenging experience and accompanying epiphany, the rationale and positive ideas that I gained in those and like situations stayed with me, gradually forming the benchmark from which I now approach all the noise of thought when it is disturbed: in peace and equanimity. The benefits of using challenging experiences to learn how to be steady in the face of the uprising of thought in this way can be incalculable.

Equally valuable, however, is learning about quietness from others. Years ago, before our company went public and we were on our own, the vice president of finance for our parent company was a good friend of mine. He lived in New York and I in California, but I often went out partying with him, and for years I observed his knack for quietness at our monthly meetings in New York. He was very well-thought-of by many, often referred to as "that brilliant guy." Yet in all our many business encounters, and there were scores of them, I never heard him say much of anything. So while he was smart, how would most people have known he was brilliant, since he had developed the skill of saying so little? Unfounded, presumptive attribution, of course.

Another person I learned the benefits of the quiet response from was a corporate lawyer. Also a bright fellow, he had mastered the art of listening and keeping his balance intact in the often useless stream of noise that goes on in meetings by responding to most of it with a mellow "uh-huh." It took me a while to see the value in what he was doing, but not a minute longer than that to begin to adopt it as part of my own daily repertoire—and not only in business, but also in other ways.

For example, before my mother died, I helped her relocate to La Jolla, where she spent the last few years of her life. I mentioned earlier that my mother was uneducated, yet quite intelligent, but I failed to mention that among the many dogmatic teachers and others like them who surrounded me in my youth, she was among the fiercest in maintaining and defending her opinions.

I was always very polite to my mother. Yet, being not without my own opinions, which often no more matched hers than they did the teachers I met from childhood onward, I frequently found myself in disagreement, and even mild contention, with her. By the time I moved her to California, however, I had determined that no matter what she said, I was going to get over my foolish need to differ with her. During the entire move, I approached her with quietness, meeting everything she said that I disagreed with, with some form of that wonderful response "Uh-huh."

From that point forward, even when I found myself at odds with what she said, I never again opposed her by saying, or even intimating, that we weren't in concert. Instead, I simply responded quietly with the kindness of "I can see how you feel that way," or more simply, "Uh-huh."

Even though I was an adult, my mother often still wanted to be the mother and, in that, the one who was always right. So I let her be. I never knew how well this was working until one day, when she and my sister and I were in my kitchen talking about something that must have seemed important and my sister asked my opinion on it, before I could respond, my mother exclaimed, "Oh, don't bother asking him. He'll just say 'uh-huh.'"

At that, I burst out laughing, and then so did she, the contention of "I'm right, which means you're wrong," gone forever from our relationship.

Refusing to Settle

The preceding examples, though simple, express a very important principle: since others usually identify themselves with their positions and by their ideas, trying to prove them wrong (other than within the framework of your assigned role in a business situation)—even when you are certain that you are right—does little but cause discord. And causing discord will accomplish no less than making both me and the other person discontent.

A basic condition of contentment is harmony. If I want harmony, I must become harmonious. And to become so, I cannot remain in conflict, not only with regards to others whose opinions I may differ with daily, but also in regards to myself, to my actions, to the results of my labor, and so on.

Said another way, outcomes—who shows up, how things turn out, and what people are dogmatic about—are fact, so opposing it or them or what they are fixated on is about as sensible as arguing with a wall.

Here are a few brief comments from the wise on meeting life as it presents itself:

The Bhagavad Gita: "One who does what must be done without concern for the fruits is a man of renunciation and discipline."[27]

Eleanor Roosevelt: "You have to accept whatever comes, and the only important thing is that you meet it with the best you have to give."[28]

Kenneth Wapnick: "We change what is inside by accepting what is outside."[29]

Epictetus: "Inner serenity is the only serenity."[30]

Although the wise are united on this matter, it took me a long time to accept such wisdom. Why? Because doing so means abandoning false hope and excessive ambition, as well as dismissing the desires and emotions that feed them. As the Dutch philosopher Baruch Spinoza said, "For a man at the mercy of his emotions is not his own master but is subject to fortune."[31]

In Plato's *Menexenus*, Socrates reminds us of the value of remaining balanced in the face of what comes when he says this:

> The old saying 'nothing too much'... really was well
> said. For he whose happiness rests with himself ... who
> is not hanging in suspense on other men or changing
> with the vicissitude of their fortune, has his life ordered
> for the best. He is temperate and valiant and wise, and
> when his riches come and go, when his children are
> given and taken away, he will remember the proverb,

'Neither rejoicing over much nor grieving over much,' for he relies on himself.[32]

In *The Perennial Philosophy*, Aldous Huxley, echoing Socrates, says:

> This is perhaps the most difficult of all mortifications— to achieve a "holy indifference" to the temporal success or failure of the cause to which one has devoted one's best energies. If it triumphs, well and good; and if it meets defeat, that is also well and good, if only in ways that, to a limited and time-bound mind, are here and now entirely incomprehensible....
>
> Sufficient not only unto the day, but also unto the place, is the evil thereof. Agitation over happenings which we are powerless to modify, either because they have not yet occurred, or else are occurring at an inaccessible distance from us, achieves nothing beyond the inoculation of here and now with the remote or anticipated evil that is the object of our distress.[33]

For me, discovering that events are simply events, that what is neutral cannot be personal, and thus, that quietness is often the best response, became lessons for a lifetime. And as I considered these ideas more carefully, the emptiness of just winning more jousts became clearer.

During this time, I headed up a second company, Continuous Curve, a contact lens company, along with my own, National Health Laboratories, for a while, but my growing power, position, and even wealth were all starting to mean less and less. That may sound like the absence of a benefit, but it was actually contributing to an enormous transformation. I had the growing realization that there was no point in striving so hard for more when I already had enough. And contrary to what many may believe, this realization didn't stop me from doing my utmost to succeed; rather, it enabled me to cease giving power to my emotional swings about the unavoidable downs that always accompany the ups in every business journey.

In addition to learning how to be indifferent about results, I learned how to discern between real satisfaction and pseudo-satisfaction. An example of pseudo-satisfaction: Say you meet the perfect person, get the big promotion, are invited to join the exclusive club, find the ideal house, or receive the highest bonus. You are fulfilled, satisfied, finally happy. Three months later a problem develops and your happiness packs up and walks out the door. Why? Because it was mere infatuation you were experiencing, not happiness at all.

So, in a world so filled with ephemeral, pseudo-joys, how do you understand what real happiness is? I think the first step is to examine the subject seriously, asking yourself the following questions: Is happiness the same as pleasure, something that can be bought in the marketplace or sought after as a prize? Is it a thing to be conferred upon you by others? Is it sorrow's temporary absence or even an impermanent cessation of pain? Is it the honeymoon period, the rest being what you have to put up with? Is happiness something variable, inconstant, and fickle?

Are you to believe those who tell you happiness is to be found when you master "the secret"? Or should you pay attention to the others who say to be humble and accept that consistent happiness is outside your power and not your proper inheritance? Shall you surrender to such thinking and put your energy into avoiding pain, looking forward to and falling into infatuation whenever possible? Or should you stand up and contend that infatuation is not nearly enough and, despite the effort required, reach for the stars and for peace eternal? Is such an outlook too much to expect? Too grandiose? Too lacking in humility or modesty?

Accepting this as your quest could mean that you will have far fewer infatuations and therefore will overlook moments of passing pleasure. It could even mean that by demanding more than just a little, you will end up with nothing at all. Or perhaps your insistence that complete contentment be yours will lead you past the transitory and fleeting and onto a satisfaction that never ends, satisfaction that will be yours for one simple reason: *because you refused to settle before you reached the end.*

8
Power

The Real Accomplishment

In the workplace, where much of the quest for traditional success takes place, power is not only part of the game; in many ways it *is* the game. Thriving in the workplace, then, is often about discovering who has the power and then using that knowledge wisely, learning not to fight the powerful—unless you have the clout to defeat them and find it necessary to do so.

In other words, your objective in relationship to power should be to find where it resides and then to live there in concert with it. The productive idea is to work with power: to flow with it as it comes, or sidestep it in graceful avoidance when you see it gathering focus against you. The alternative, fighting with others or holding contentions and complaints against those in power, serves only to retard your progress.

This doesn't mean that you should seek out those who are powerful and hang onto them, however. It means, simply, that you should learn to remain balanced in your outlook regardless of the machinations of the power politics that constantly swirl around you. How? By being content with yourself and your personal power, without need for anything else.

Plato, the *I Ching,* and others like them counsel that to gain the power that we all intrinsically seek, we should focus on becoming stronger within, because the power we are looking for does not lie in the ability to hire and fire, or to be noticed or praised; it lies in the ability to no longer care about either your own position in relation to that of others or even what they think.

How do you get this healthier outlook on life and the opinions of others? Most likely you are quite familiar with what you believe is your weakness and your concerns about your image. But to find power within yourself to not care about what you can't control, you will need to become reacquainted with your strength. Once you welcome its return, or better said, your return to it, it will allow you to question your anxieties and brush aside your convictions of personal frailty. As you become free of such debilitating barriers to certainty, you will begin to see yourself in a more kindly light and wonder how you ever let the darkness of doubt have its way with you for so long.

Now let's consider a different scenario: what if you are the one in your organization who has the power? Or what if you become one of the powerful? Then you must learn something else: to become wise enough to use the power you are granted appropriately; that is, you must learn not to abuse it, despite the ever-present temptations to do so. Consider this story about the feared and powerful former FBI director J. Edgar Hoover and the Mafia from the book *Double Cross* by Sam and Chuck Giancana (the man named Mooney is Sam Giancana himself):

> Mooney also confided that J. Edgar Hoover himself had been on the pad for years. "[Frank] Costello worked the whole thing out. He knew Hoover was just like every other politician and copper, only meaner and smarter than most. Hoover didn't want an envelope each month—that offended his sensibilities," Mooney

said, sneering. "So we never gave him cash outright; we gave him something better. Tips on fixed horse races. It was up to him how much money he wanted to make on the information. He could bet ten thousand dollars on a horse that showed twenty-to-one odds, if he wanted ... and he has."

Getting the tips to Hoover was easy enough, Mooney explained. Frank Costello would hear from Frank Erikson, the country's biggest and most powerful bookie, about an upcoming fix on a race. Next, Costello would tell columnist Walter Winchell, and Winchell, in turn, would call Hoover. Hoover would hop in his car under the pretext he was working on a case and head for the track.

"He'd place a two-dollar bet at the window while one of his flunkies put the real money on the sure thing at the hundred-dollar window," Mooney said. He told Chuck [Giancana—the son] that Costello never let the FBI director down; Hoover won every time.[34]

If this is true, it is a great cautionary tale about the temptations that accompany power, even for the best of us. For all those who abuse power will sooner or later pay dearly. Why? Because power follows the rule of physics that says for every action there is an equal and opposite reaction; that is, the usage of power always has a reaction on the user. Simply put, power, when misused, weakens and corrupts. Or, at the least, its abuse leaves you feeling guilty and anxious, and here I speak from long experience, like many, having made numerous mistakes in the misuse of power both at work and at home.

In a nutshell, gaining the power you really want—power accompanied by a quiet certainty—lies in remembering your ability to remain at peace, regardless of externals. Keeping the power you have—that same quiet kind—lies in respecting it enough not to abuse it, this, above all, making a difficult life worth living.

Who Is Invincible?

Epictetus said this about the power we possess to deal positively with all we face:

> First clearly understand that every event is indifferent and nothing to you, whatever sort it may be. For it will be in your power to make a right use of it, and this, no one can hinder. To me, all portents are lucky if I will them to be. For whatever happens, it belongs to me to derive advantage therefrom.... Demand not that events should happen as you wish, but wish them to happen as they do happen and your life will be serene....
>
> Who then is invincible? He whom the inevitable cannot overcome.... Can I say to the inevitable that it is nothing to me?[35]

In your life, can you say to the problems you encounter, "You are nothing to me" in this same way? Of course you can! But being able to do so requires your commitment to lay down your regrets about the past as well as your worries about the future, and then to pick up a new way of living, one in which you decide for this: a continual noncontentious engagement with the "what is" of your life. Fortunately, this way of life is not only possible but already yours, just waiting for your acceptance.

Remember when the Wizard of Oz showed the Scarecrow, the Tin Man, and the Cowardly Lion that they already had a brain, a heart, and courage? And then Dorothy learned that she was safe at home in Kansas and just dreaming she was in danger? None of them gained anything new. They were just finally able to see that they already possessed what they had been searching for. And yet, without a little encouragement from the wizard, together with a somewhat harrowing journey, they may not have been able to see it.

Likewise, learning how to have great trust in yourself—which you also get from a challenging personal journey and some self-encouragement—is what will enable you to see what is already there and belongs to you. Such self-trust will allow you to live in the present in a way that people often talk glibly about but rarely accomplish. And it is at this point—when you realize that every disturbance that seems to come from without is nothing but the shadow of your decision to remove yourself from the power to be at peace within—that your need for a complicated formula for living disappears.

Think about it this way for a moment. Every business problem passes. Therefore, every problem you face at work is in the process of dissolution from the moment it arrives. Since this is so, what lasting import can it have? No matter what you may believe to the contrary, you are the strong one in every seeming contest against this or that blustering phantom with no permanent reality. Yet for you to become aware of this truth, you must begin to withdraw from every thought that defines appearances as powerful and yourself as weak or needy.

"But wait a minute," you might anxiously say, "my problem is not just an appearance, but something really serious." No, it is not. Why? Because it is leaving, departing, and will soon be gone, and therefore cannot be nearly as serious as a frightened mind might believe.

A final thing to accept is that you do not change the nature of a circumstance when you oppose it or worry it through, even when it appears to change because of your efforts. Its true nature is not discovered in its changing forms, but only in the fact it is impermanent. This is what never changes: meeting the challenge, doing your best to resolve the issue, and refusing to overly revisit it after it leaves ends your part in every matter. The rest is vain preoccupation.

Respect

The basic idea at your place of work is that your boss has a picture he or she wants you to paint. If you are to go beyond the painful consequences of resistance, you must see that your function is not to ask "Why?" or "Why me?" Your function is simply to ask "What color, what size, and how long should it take?"

Let us say that at the end of the week you turn in a project you have worked hard on, and when you arrive at work on Monday, the boss throws it back to you with a comment that essentially says, "This is unsatisfactory." Your first reaction would probably be something like, "But I worked so hard on that." (That may or may not be true, because when it comes to self-protection, the untamed mind is prone to exaggeration, rationalization, and a certain amount of duplicity.) Your second and equally disturbed reaction might be, "Who needs this? Maybe I should just leave and find a job where my good efforts will be appreciated."

On the other hand, if you have come to the point of learning how to release yourself from reacting in those first two ways, your common sense will enter and help you say to yourself, "Wait just a moment. I want to think this through before I act or even speak. Perhaps the boss is right. Maybe this is not my best work. I know from experience that it's possible for me to do less than my best at times. Perhaps I missed something because I was tired or distracted. Or perhaps the boss is oppressed by personal problems, and in her pain she is taking it out on me. Or perhaps this project influences another one that my boss is aware of that I am not."

After pausing to consider more reasonable explanations— possibly in a flash—you can respond reasonably. You can say, in one fashion or another, "Sorry boss, I thought I did okay on it, but please tell me how you want it improved and I will get on it right away."

Right or wrong, good report or bad, her problem or yours, it makes no difference. In choosing a reasonable response, you have quietly taken the wind, at least as it relates to you, out of her sails. And unless she is a terrible person or in terrible trouble, your decision to stand aside from the uselessness of complaint and to cooperate instead means that you have won the day.

The reason that I stress cooperation, accepting what comes without complaint and living fully in your present assignments, is that only such a life can be peaceful and worthy. To live without the burden of fighting with those in power is the sign of maturity. As difficult as it may at times appear to be, your responsibility is to support those you work for in the very same way that you should support the heads of your family. This doesn't mean that you always agree with them; it means that you always respect their right to their position. The alternative is to engage in power struggles with authority figures for no good reason.

The point of all this is to come out of the confusion that is reinforced by unnecessary contention and to learn the proper use of power, that power may be robbed of its power to use you. Why is this so important? Because when you fight with it, you feed its raw nature, giving it the opening it needs to turn and feed on you.

These are not just ideas about one more subject in your already busy life, but cautions about what has a direct, albeit at times unconscious, effect on you. In an aggressive world like business, where one has become conditioned to an aggressive approach to almost everything, it seems to take forever to learn that the goal of a respectful cooperation must precede action, if the action is to have value to you. If not, you will be forced to perceive employees as chattels, co-workers as competitors, and bosses as enemies, thereby destroying the balanced perspective that emerges from your side of a "properly powerful" relationship.

Kindness Is Remembered

Learning about power and its uses and misuses in this world begins for all of us at an early age, first with our parents, and then with others. The day my family arrived in the Bronx, I met my first playmate, an older boy who lived in the same building. We played a game called airplane. But somehow, to my growing consternation, in his perception he won every game. This, as I came to learn, would carry over into just about every relationship that I had on the streets with bigger or more powerful boys, and into those with greater powers at church and school, including the all-powerful principal, whose face, I still remember, contorted with rage as she beat my hands with a ruler. Not until years later did I understand that the poor woman's distorted applications of power had nothing to do with me or the other children, but only with her own terrible fears.

Such was my parochial education. My third-grade teacher went berserk on a regular basis and was eventually "sent away." My sixth- and eighth-grade teachers, both furious and mean, but one coldly and the other hotly so, would have greatly benefited from a compassionate retreat or, perhaps even more, from rehabilitation; their suffering was apparent in their every hateful deed. As for the priests, they were, in the main, lost. In their addled thinking, they were specially selected and anointed emissaries of God to man, the so-called religious, leaving the rest of us as what, I wondered? The irreligious?

Yet, like my fourth-grade teacher, who was a saint, there were some helpful exceptions. In the hierarchy of our neighborhood, where the few people with either an education or a little money were granted a certain respect, and where the powerful ruled the streets with hard fists, no one, and I mean no one, commanded more fearsome reverence than the monsignor who headed the church and school. This indisputable heavyweight champion of the neighborhood thundered forth weekly from the pulpit and, because he was hard of hearing, also from the confessional, leaving the pews leading to his confessional sparsely populated while others were packed. He wasn't mean, but he was a smart and tough disciplinarian, held in awe by all. And he was a man who taught me an important lesson in the proper use of power.

Every year, the school held a fundraising bazaar with cake sales, games of chance, and the like. In the eighth grade, when I was on the edge of the zone of recklessness where I spent the following few years, I worked the counter at one of the games. Already a bit sneaky, I had occasionally, in times before, taken things that didn't belong to me. Yet, for some reason, the situation that day seemed like a golden opportunity for a poor boy to enrich himself without much effort or risk. With this in mind, I began surreptitiously to make it one quarter for them and one for me, carefully slipping "mine" into the back pocket of my jeans.

This covert activity went on for quite a while, until just about the time I had my pocket pretty well filled. And then who should come walking through the crowd—which parted for him like the Red Sea—checking the action and heading directly for me, but that terrible symbol of authority, the universally feared monsignor.

Now, in general, I wasn't all that afraid of him. Having daily been around the church and school and rectory from the time I was six, and he being my dad's boss, I knew him well enough, and was, if you will, used to him. However, at that moment, with a pocketful of stolen money, and "his" money at that, I was terrified. My palms began to ooze those cold drops of dread. My brow and neck became equally clammy. I was deeply shaken, not only at the thought that he would discover my perfidy, but that he, who could be quite vocal and forceful, would expose me publicly for the thief that I, at the moment, certainly was. My mind raced, picturing the most terrible scenarios: him yelling and me leaving the crowded bazaar with my head hanging down in shame; the gossips of the neighborhood having a field day with my criminal behavior; my parents reacting explosively. Then, just as my imagination started to brim with such despairing thoughts, the fearsome one turned and was lost in the crowd.

If sighs of relief could move mountains, mine relocated the Rockies to Florida. With my frightened prayer answered, I gladly went back to my duties, no longer stealing—although not putting back, mind you—I was too greedy for that.

In my business with all the people in front of me, I forgot about what had happened and stopped noticing much else around me. About fifteen minutes later, someone walked up behind me and gently, but firmly, tapped my bulging back pocket. After I jumped a couple of inches off the ground, I turned around to see who had touched me, and the person walking away was, of course, the monsignor. He had not made a fuss. He had not told me to put it back. He had, in fact, not uttered a sound; he had simply tapped my pocket and then moved on without even looking back. I spent the next half-hour quietly putting back what I had taken, amazed at my good fortune and grateful beyond measure. And while the monsignor and I met numerous times thereafter, he never mentioned it, and I never expressed my gratitude to him for what he had done.

Yet in some ways I did thank him, in fact over and over and over again, in my every remembrance of his kindness, when I let its generosity, which remained in my heart, help me be generous toward others. His act was a simple but vivid demonstration of the proper use of power, a telling example of how, when married to kindness, it can have an effect on another person that lasts a lifetime. I never had the ideal of a grandfather in my life, but if a boy can love a man for his goodness, I loved that feared man, as he showed in the quietness of his action that he loved me.

This is a lesson far-reaching in value. To let people off the hook, especially when you have the goods on them and the power to keep them there, is beneficial not only for them and for the rest of us, but above all, for you.

9

The Desire for Illusions

Questioning Certainty

A person on the way to true success must shed another problematic habit: the ridiculous need to be always right. The importance of this principle is well illustrated in a book I read many years ago, *Actualizations: You Don't Have to Rehearse to Be Yourself.* This book by Stewart Emery presents lessons about being fair in considering the beliefs of others. In one example, the author asked his readers to envision the following scenario as a "serious" difference of opinion: Two people stand opposite from each other in the corners of a room filled with a giant beach ball. Because the ball fills the room completely, each person can only see the color of the beach ball on his own side. For example, one person sees that it is red on his side but cannot see that it is blue on the other.[36]

This person begins by saying, "The beach ball is red." The other counters with, "No, the beach ball is blue." The first follows with, "Hey, take a closer look. It's not blue, it's red." The other responds with, "Hey, you look closer, silly. The beach ball is blue." The first follows with, "Me? Silly? Hey, stupid, anyone can see that the beach ball is red." The other comes back with, "Now look here, you insufferable boor …"

You get the point.

What is the solution for such a conundrum? To go over to the other person's side and look at it from his viewpoint. From there, you can see that the beach ball is blue. And even if you can see blue from no other position than there, and thus still conclude that the answer to the problem is red, you also can no longer insist the other person is wrong.

Illegitimate arguments, and every argument is illegitimate, attack your certainty. Why? Because in every argument, somewhere inside yourself, you know that you are half of the problem and that if you would simply stop arguing, the whole problem, at least for you, would blow away. Similarly, to grow in business you must learn to question not only your conviction in the veracity of your own viewpoint, but also the often dogmatic nature of the status quo.

It reminds me of a story I once heard Kenneth Wapnick tell about a great sage who brought his students together each morning for meditation. Their only problem was his pet cat, which would prowl around disturbing their quietness. They solved this problem, at the sage's instruction, by beginning each day's ritual by tying the cat to a post. After many years the sage passed on, but his disciples continued this daily ritual. Years later, the cat also died. The next day the disciples went out and purchased another cat, which the following morning they tied to the post, because that is the way it had always been done.

That may seem like just another silly story until you begin to examine your life at work and consider how many strange things you or your company may do simply because "that's the way it has always been done." Unfortunately, many businesspeople are unquestioning conformists, caught in habitual patterns of thinking and behavior, taking the status quo for granted, and accepting themselves as they are: mindless cogs in a machine bent on avarice, molded in the machine's version of what they should be.

If you shy away from a rigorous examination of your thinking and of the traditional methods and values of business, you restrict yourself to the limited horizons of commonly accepted thought. This leads nowhere. If you are to succeed at undoing your limitations, you do not blindly accept—you query.

Collateral Damage

As you look about your world carefully, it will become more and more evident that companies are often self-centered, shortsighted, dishonest, and cruel. This means that the people who run these companies are often self-centered, shortsighted, dishonest, and cruel. Is this because they are naturally that way? Or is it because the part of their thinking that enjoys the kill has been allowed free rein for so long that it has become dominant, and that the harmful behavior that comes from such thinking has become so ingrained and habitually "natural" as a response that the only time they get in touch with what they are doing is in their worst nightmares?

Think of the mentality that led to "caveat emptor" and what that did to the relationship between the customer and the company. Now transfer that thinking to the company and its employees and see how their relationship, too, has turned into one of mistrust: Mistrust on the part of the employees brought about by the deceptive practices of management. Mistrust on the part of management, fearing their evil intentions will boomerang.

How has this come about? How have we so lost our bearings? Is it that through years of these practices we have become so accustomed to heartless terms like *collateral damage* that as long as the damage does not appear to affect us directly, we no longer care what happens to others? Is it that at the top, the air becomes so rarified that those in charge think, due to the lack of "oxygen," the rules of decency no longer apply? Have the self-serving seekers of more profit who proclaim that "outsourcing creates jobs" actually come to believe their lies?

The confused adherents of the misguided notion that the survival of the fittest will produce a stronger organization do not understand that the world of business cannot prosper over the long run if employees continue to be seen as serfs and the higher-ups as lords of the manor with an inherited right to take as they will. True egalitarianism, the only thing that can save those in power from themselves, does not require a redistribution of wealth, but only the cessation of plundering and the protection of those who cannot protect themselves, which is the responsibility of every manager and owner alike.

Only fairness will lead to peace of mind, and it is this you seek, not reaching peak after peak on a mountain with no top. When you consider this deeply, you may find your heart sinking as you ask yourself, "But what about all the effort I expended in getting here?" Yet if you have been doing nothing more thus far than vainly climbing Mount Nowhere, the answer to your sense of loss is that there is no loss in leaving a path that leads nowhere, the recognition of this becoming your immediate gain.

When you have found even the fringes of true peace of mind, you do not regret having spent so much time in illusions of satisfaction. How else could your friend Disappointment have found you, tapped you on the shoulder, and pointed you in the direction of a better way? Seeing this, you understand that the ultimate value of a meaningless game is found only in the unvarnished recognition of its emptiness, because this alone can give you cause to decide to look elsewhere.

The Search for Truth

Obviously, shelter, warmth, safety, and financial security are not meaningless, unless you sell your character to purchase them. Beyond these basics, however, the rest of what we so often chase after is just frivolity and restlessness.

Look anywhere and you will see people with burning desires for what they confuse with success. In the cities, kids who play basketball just well enough dream that one day they will make it to the NBA. In the towns, young men who play golf just well enough convince themselves they will get through the mini-tour or qualifying school and go onto the main tour. In the world of business, numerous young scramblers hope beyond hope that fame and fortune will be right around the corner, even though the corners they have already turned led them only to more; even more pitiful, their intense focus on capturing the brass ring means they are not even enjoying the ride.

Experienced explorers, having been singed by the emptiness and despair of common achievement, understand that success means finding truth, and that the only place that truth exists is *within ourselves*.

In Plato's *Republic*, Socrates says:

> Would it surprise you if men without experience of truth and reality hold unsound opinions about many matters? In this way then, consider it: are not hunger and thirst emptiness of the bodily habit? And is not ignorance and folly in turn a kind of emptiness...? Then those who have no experience of wisdom and virtue but are ever devoted to feastings and that sort of thing are swept downward, it seems, and back again to the center, and so sway and roam to and fro throughout their lives. But they have never transcended all this and turned their eyes to the true upper region, nor have been wafted there, nor ever been really filled with real things, nor ever tasted stable and pure pleasure. But with eyes ever bent upon the earth and heads bowed down over their tables they feast like cattle, grazing and copulating, ever greedy for more of these delights, and in their greed kicking and butting one another with horns and hoofs of iron they slay one another in sateless

avidity because they are vainly striving to satisfy with things that are not real.[37]

As for us, what could be less real than the cotton candy-like prizes of the game that evaporate as you seize them? You must slow down long enough to ask yourself why you work so hard to secure them, what enchants you so about them, why you overdo and outdo to gain them. I cannot count the number of times I purchased art, objects, and sundry other things for no better reason than they caught my eye; the many occasions I ordered new cars while the old ones were still young because I believed the acquisition would offer me more than momentary pleasure. That is where "repetition compulsion" comes in. I, like many, worked for years partially to buy bigger or fancier versions of what I had already found incapable of providing contentment.

Why do people convince themselves that they must overdo for the greater good of the company and the family? Is it not more likely that they overdo for themselves? And why do people try so hard to overachieve? After all, *over*, like *under*, is the description of a state not in balance.

Is it the gnawing need of personal pride that causes so many businesspeople to act this way? Or is it that overwork and its exhausted sleep is a chosen distraction from facing the mind's discontent? Or is fear the motivator, the overwork an attempt to manipulate the boss, an insurance policy against discharge? Or is overwork perhaps a means of desire, used to reach a more concrete end, maybe one day that great and grand prize: authorization for and use of the plane?

Don't misunderstand me, however. Overwork is not the same as hard work well done. Overwork is work overdone, essentially inefficient, and, in the long run, counterproductive. And any boss who demands this of people on a regular basis is not a good boss at all, just another thief of people's time for his or her own benefit. Even sadder is when bad work habits become an addiction, leaving the people engaging in them at a loss when they are "deprived" of their accustomed doses of seriousness, labor, and strife.

However, recognizing such addiction in yourself is no reason to cease working hard or trying to get ahead, or even to leave the world of business altogether. Rather, it is a good reason to celebrate your beginning insightfulness and, therefore, to stay. After all, why abandon your class before learning all that it has to teach? Even if all you have learned thus far is to look on the senselessness of the great contest without shrinking from what you perceive, you have come a long way indeed.

The Gate Marked "No Return"

In the book *Everest—The West Ridge* by Thomas Hornbein, there is a quote attributed to Dag Hammarskjold, the Swedish U.N. Secretary General in the 1950s, about using senselessness to benefit yourself. In describing the reasons he found not to quit before the finish, he said, "Never let success hide its emptiness from you, achievement its nothingness, toil its desolation. And so keep alive the incentive to push on further that pain in the soul which drives us beyond ourselves. Whither? That I don't know. That I don't ask to know."[38]

Kathy Galloway's poem "Going Over" describes the values you find and the difficulties you encounter on the journey to becoming your own person this way:

> You have burned your bridges.
> You have passed through the gate marked 'no return'
> and for you there's no going back.
> No going back to the security of the known, familiar house,
> to the well-known dispensations and the threadbare coverings.
>
> Now you are out there in uncharted territory
> heavy with threat and shadows not yet entered.

The risks are high, and yet you strike out boldly,
guided only by unwavering conviction
and the longing for the true centre of the land.
This is what it means to do a new thing.

So, you travel lightly.
You are abandoned, given up in all things
to the task that lies ahead.
Therefore, you may be exactly who you are.
You have inhabited yourself,
you are at home,
and home is where you are,
even if it is a desert.
No one can dispossess you of your own in-dwelling.
This is what it means to be free.

We stand, one foot upon the bridge,
wondering if we too have the courage to go over
and strike the match behind us.[39]

Putting your foot on the bridge comes with discovering that your present position, no matter its seeming status or lack thereof, contains the potential to help you uncover the lies that have been whispering slanderous tales about the devaluation of your inestimable worth. In other words, if you are lost behind the agonizing curtain of shame and self-doubt, if you see your mistakes as crimes and your faults as permanent, instead of as knots in a string, there simply to be undone, then accepting the potential that lies in your current job function is a requirement; it is the key that will unlock the doorway leading out of this painful world of misplaced ambition and, more importantly, worry about what you cannot control.

In summary, *the sunset of being swept up in the importance of your career is actually this: the dawn of the realization of the importance of your life.*

PART III

LIFE

10

The Two Worlds

The Last of Human Freedoms

Life is of the mind, in the mind, and ultimately, in your experience of it, nowhere else. For example, my wife Kathy and I meet someone. She likes this person; I do not. Later things change. She no longer thinks the person is so great; I think the person is pretty nice. Or, let's say we go to a movie. Kathy likes it, but I don't. We listen to music. She doesn't care for it, but I do. Why is this so? Because we come from different backgrounds and experiences, are subject to different moods at any given time, and have formed different values, tastes, opinions, and beliefs, all of which are changeable.

Think of it this way. When you open your eyes in the morning, you awaken to two worlds. The first is the world of facts through which you wend your way and often wander. The second is the world of interpretation, the one in which you actually live. If you think about it carefully, you will realize that every appearance that greets you, no matter its form, is empty of meaningful content *for* you until it is supplied *by* you. This means that every letter or document you receive, in its influence and effect, is your writing to yourself. Every call that comes in is what you say it is to you. Every problem you encounter is what you define it to be. You are peering outward into every situation as if into a mental mirror, perceiving the reflection of what you have chosen—consciously or not—the situation to be to you.

Accepting this intellectually is one thing; learning to live with it as the centerpiece of your relationships with people and circumstances, quite another. Yet if you want to find freedom from those twin fetters of the mind, victimhood and blame, this is exactly what you must learn.

An extreme but classic example of this idea is found in Victor Frankl's book, *Man's Search for Meaning*, in which he describes how, in the darkest pit of a concentration camp, where only one out of twenty-seven survived, some men showed him the real power of the mind. He wrote:

> We who lived in concentration camps can remember the men who walked through the huts comforting others, giving away their last pieces of bread. They may have been few in number, but they offered sufficient proof that everything can be taken from a man but one thing: the last of the human freedoms—to choose one's attitude in any given set of circumstances, to choose one's own way. [40]

No one controls the inevitable and sometimes piteous unfoldings of the objective world. If, however, you are willing to work at it, you can begin to take charge of your subjective world. Once you have had the experience of becoming really upset over something and staying with the turmoil of it long enough to realize that the source of the distress lay not where you had thought, but in your own misperception, you are on your way. Like the child in swimming lessons who was afraid of the water and yet one day finally plunged in and swam across the pool, you have overcome your fear, dived in, and reached the other side of irresponsibility about perception and emotion. Next time you have to plunge in, you may be nervous again, even afraid of what you've accomplished so far, and you may wait a while before giving it a second try; but that's no matter—once you've accomplished it, you've accomplished it. One day, you'll certainly remember that is true and do so again.

This persistence in face of fear is how you remember your strength and dismiss your conviction of littleness, the way to find reason for hope even when things are turning out in a direction exactly opposite to the way you had wished for and envisioned.

I'm Doing This to Myself

One of Webster's definitions for *mind* is "all of an individual's conscious experiences."[41] Yet, as I have pointed out, the experiences that helped form my opinions, beliefs, memories, and thinking, were subjective. I viewed them through the lenses of my then *state of mind* and the information I possessed, or lacked. Again, fortunately, all of those interpretations are now subject to my reconsideration and changeable at will. Unfortunately, the actual task of changing your interpretations is usually much harder to do than it may sound. It takes great willingness and time to learn that "It's not my fault; it's yours" is a deception, and that "I'm doing this to myself" is the truth.

For me, it took many experiences of taking one step at a time—some steps bigger than others. Each lesson in personal responsibility helped me pay that much more attention to my thinking and thereby understand that much more about myself.

One seemingly minor experience that had a profound impact on me was being miserable in the presidential suite of a great hotel in Hawaii. This misery illuminated a problem in my outlook. A problem that, as I looked on it with a new perspective, I was able to resolve, and that reminded me I could do this with everything.

With fresh eyes, I remembered a teacher who had tormented me, which helped me to forgive myself for allowing her to have power over me and to forgive her for what she didn't do to take my power away. I revisited my relationships with those whom I had chosen as enemies, which made it clear how wrong I had been and allowed me to apologize in my mind to each of them.

By this time, I began to see that my difficulties with my father, my teachers, the army, and the like were completely caused by my own fabricated versions of each situation I was in. In none of those situations did anyone ask me to do anything particularly different from what others were required to do; I just didn't want to do what was required. I wanted the independence of the immature, on my own childish terms. In fact, I can remember once feeling a rush within myself over my freedom to refuse to do what I was told and, instead, do what I wanted; it happened as I was walking past a chain gang one morning in Georgia on my way to what I thought would be my doing whatever I chose to do in Florida. As if I knew what freedom meant at fifteen.

With my growing willingness to reconsider my opinions, I started to see everything and everyone differently. I looked back at the time when the head of a large organization invited me, when I was young, to sit by the window of his fancy office overlooking Central Park, and then charmed me over coffee and biscuits. As I thought about this, I saw clearly that he did so not because he cared for me, but because he wanted something from me, and charming me was his way of getting it. This realization led me to remember other times when people paid me handsomely for something I had accomplished, again not because of anything personal, but simply because they wanted greater performance from me next time. *None* of it was personal; none of the praise and, as I eventually learned, equally, none of the blame.

Even as a child, however, I must have had some notion that everything is in the mind. I can remember asking a friend whether my first girlfriend was pretty or not, because I knew, liking her as I did, I couldn't see her as she was. I also remember talking to another friend about the trance-like state brought on by puppy love and his telling me of his method for escaping the bondage it seemed to impose upon him. He said that when he no longer wanted to be in such a condition, he would find some flaw in the girl he was enraptured by, exaggerate it greatly, and from then on focus only on that. Crude, perhaps, but effective, he said, in returning him to greater control over himself. He, too, had realized that it was all in his mind—and since it was therefore subject to him, he needed not remain subject to it.

How Smart Was I?

What follows is another minor, but good, example of what I mean about being deceived by the mind's trickiness. Years ago, I occasionally played golf with a fellow who had the habit of exclaiming, right as the ball left the clubface, "Oh, that one is in trouble!" At the time, I was young enough and foolish enough to let such petty things annoy me, and so I was, on the golf course, that is, inclined to look on him critically. One day, during a round of golf, I had an "important" shot, during which he coughed. I missed the shot and was internally furious at him for causing me to do so.

In this situation, I made two mistakes. My first was believing that his cough generated my distress. My predisposition to look at him negatively on the golf course, my foolish belief that the shot was important, my upset at missing it, and my then bad habit of listening to instead of watching my mind's fits of spite, all combined to distort my understanding of the experience. My second and more insidious mistake, however, lay in my misperception of the actual order of events; not until that evening did I realize he had coughed *after* I hit my shot.

It took me a while after that to adjust to the idea that perception is the result of a decision and, therefore, that each of us is responsible for what we perceive and how we feel. In that light, would it have made a difference if the guy *had* coughed during my shot? Not if I was aware that how I felt about it came from me. But I was not aware, and paradoxically, the incident happened in a time of great business success, when I would have told you, and believed, how clearly I could see and how smart I was.

Here is another brief example. One Friday evening during a business trip to New York, Kathy and I were at our hotel, dressing for dinner, which was to be followed by an evening at a hit Broadway play. As we were about to leave, a call came in from one of my general managers. He gave me the unwelcome news that a senior scientist from one of our laboratories, a man I had recently been kind to in part because of his family problems, had abruptly resigned to join a competitor. The competitor was run by another fellow who had once worked for me, someone whom I had also been considerate to when he had experienced some personal problems.

I instantly (although it is never that rapid, since there must always be time to make the decision to leave the calmness that accompanies good sense) became furious over what I saw as their betrayal. And captured by my choice to be fearful about what the loss would mean to the company—and, therefore, to me—the still immature part of my mind began to rant and rave over the double-dealing nature of these two dirty so-and-so's. I wanted to exclude them from the ranks of those worthy of life, liberty, and the pursuit of their own happiness. And as the night progressed, my rage grew fiercer. While I tried to cover it with a good face, I am sure I was a less-than-charming dinner companion. The upset still did not let up in the limo and rolled on relentlessly through the play, about which the only thing I remember is that I did not much like it. By bedtime, I was no better.

In other words, I lost it. No matter what excuses I may have concocted, such as being overtired, under great stress, or whatever, the fact remained that I was not, at that moment, what I should have been: a leader dealing effectively with one of the waves of conflict that come and go in the daily contest of business. Rather than taking responsibility for my pitiful condition, as I should have done, I allowed myself to slip and fall into anger, to become a petulant child, whining and blaming others for treating me unfairly and making my evening unhappy.

The next day, but only after I had spent a number of hellish hours in the mistaken belief that I could be betrayed emotionally by someone other than myself, I straightened myself out. Once I was again rational, I could ask and answer the question, "What really happened?"

First, the fellow who ran the competing company was not doing nearly as well as we were and so was trying to raid us for talent. My being nice to him in prior days did not, could not, and should not have meant that he was obligated to be nice to me in return. He was a businessman trying to survive the only way he knew how. I'd have done the same.

Likewise, the scientist who took the offer was just trying to thrive. Because I had gone out of my way for him and treated him well, should he have called me before accepting the other man's offer? Perhaps. Yet perhaps he did not call because the other fellow made him promise not to. Or perhaps he believed the new job would lead to greater things for him and did not want to be talked out of leaving. In either case, what did his behavior have to do with the way I was choosing to look at it? Absolutely nothing. (As an aside, about eighteen months later, he asked to return, and because he was a good man, we logically, rationally, and gladly welcomed him back.)

What is the moral of this story? I made another mistake, another wrong choice. I let my kindness to someone assume the false posture of an obligation due, which means I had given a gift with strings attached. Therefore, I had not given a gift at all. The cost to me for my duplicity? The pain of self-betrayal replaced the enjoyment of what was meant to be a lovely evening with my wife.

In the final analysis, nothing all that earth-shaking happened in this example or in any of my numerous other misunderstandings.

Each situation, because I was willing to learn from it, was a lesson about taking responsibility for sight and emotion.

In this way, to learn from our mistakes is to see through the superficial chatter of the mind that says either, "You are such a stupid fool" or "Someone else made you do it," to the quietness that tells you, "The sole purpose of this painful episode is to teach you not to repeat it." And this message holds true for isolated errors as well as mistakes you repeat scores of times before you cease to hurt yourself in that particular fashion.

It's kind of like a man who drinks to excess. If, when he reaches drink number 10,000, he tells himself, "This is ridiculous, and I refuse to do it any longer," and he quits, the 9,999 drinks that led him to the last one all become good. Why? Because that was *his* way of reaching sobriety, and now that he is there, who cares any longer *how* he got there. Sure, he may have to get back on track, repay some debts, save some money, and get back in shape, but that's all piddling stuff compared to the fact that he is, at last, sober. He (if he cares for himself) and anyone else who cares for him will see that this is the only important point and let the rest go.

So it is with all mistakes. Once you cease making a mistake, you have ceased making it. Therefore, aside from saying you are sorry or making amends, and, obviously, being vigilant about not slipping into what led you to make the mistake to begin with—whether it be a particular situation or an old, familiar habit—you are done. And when your wrong-mindedness tells you this is not so, that you should walk around forever in misery lamenting, "Oh, how could I have been so evil, so stupid, so foolish," look that uselessness in the eye with a little smile and that ultimately important attitude of "Says who?"

11

The Rules of Confusion

Cheating Cheats the Cheater

In most areas of life, using common sense is necessary and good. It is wise to go on green and stop on red. It is appropriate to sit up straight when you are in a restaurant. It is bad form to pick your nose in public. And when your belief system says to follow common sense, generally, you should listen. Yet, as the programmer or boss of that belief system, which you alone have constructed, you should also become astute enough to question its advice whenever it suggests you do something likely to be unrewarding.

For example, when you find your mind saying things like, "Don't take that lying down. Be a man and strike back twice as hard" or "It's okay to be sloppy on this; it's just a small matter" or "Why should you care if you're disturbing others with your attitude? You're hurting, and so what if they hurt, too?" you should respond only with doubt, saying to your self-developed thought system, "Listen here. I made you. You didn't make me. Therefore, you have no power to dictate what I do."

In my experience of such senselessness at work, the made-up rules I found most damaging to progress—either personal or professional—are the Four Rules of Confusion.

Rule 1: Others are unlike me, their needs being different and less important than my own.

If you look at the world through self-loving eyes, you will always find what you consider to be good reasons for selfishness. In reality, though, reason and selfishness cannot coexist. Therefore, "reasons" for selfishness are reason's opposite, twisted viewpoints emanating from a crooked source. Think about it: How can anyone succeed in a process that begins by thinking less of another's rights? Can putting an equal's needs in second place ever end in lasting gain?

In his book *Cowboys, Gamblers & Hustlers*, Byron "Cowboy" Wolford tells of his experiences and the people he met in the worlds of poker, rodeos, and scam artists. In one section, he focuses on a renowned hustler named Titanic Thompson, who he says is smart as a fox and "one of the best proposition men that ever lived."[42] He then goes on to regale the reader with tales of old "Ty" hustling people at pool, bowling, horseshoes, golf, cards, and the like. Here's one of those stories:

> Then there was the deal with the "poker psychic." Ty would be sitting around a poker joint that he'd never been to before and say, "Hey guys, I know this woman who's a psychic. I'll tell you just how good she is. You take a card out of the deck and put it on the table in front of us. She doesn't live in the state, but I'll bet if you go call her she'll tell you what the card is." Back then there wasn't any TV, no short wave stuff, and Ty had been right there with them all the time, hadn't gone anywhere. Mighty near anybody would go for that deal.
>
> Then he would bet $1,000 that if they called this woman who was a psychic she could tell them over the

telephone exactly what the card was. Somebody would take a card and put it on the table. "OK," Ty would say, "here's the long distance number. Just ask for Miss Brown." They'd call and say, "Is Miss Brown there?"

"Just a moment," someone would answer. In a minute another voice said, "Hello?"

"Miss Brown, we're down here in so-and-so and we've got a bet on. This gentleman says you are quite a psychic."

"I think I am," she'd say.

"Well, we've taken a card out of the deck and laid it in the middle of the table and he bet that you could tell us what card it is."

"Give me a moment," she'd answer. Then after a short pause she'd say, "The four of diamonds," and the guy would almost faint dead away. Of course Ty had a different name for every card in the deck. If it was the four of diamonds he'd tell them to ask for Miss Brown. If it were the nine of hearts it might be Miss Ruby.[43]

Here is another deception that Cowboy recalled:

Ty was always looking for an angle. He could figure out more propositions than anyone alive. For example, while he was in Wyoming playing poker there, he and another guy drove together about twenty miles every day to the game, which was out in the desert somewhere. Every day they drove past a big rock that sat along the side of the road. "Boy, there's some big rocks in this country, ain't there?" Ty said. "Just look at all them rocks. That rock right there is a helluva rock, ain't it?"

"Yeah, yeah. There's a lot of rocks out here," the guy said, kind of bored.

The next day when they passed the boulder, Ty asked, "Wonder how much a rock like that weighs?"

"Hell, I don't know," the guy answered.

"Well, I was just wondering," Ty said.

The next morning Ty hired a man to take a truck out to the desert, load the rock on a flatbed, carry it back to town and weigh it, and then return it to its spot by the side of the road.

A few days later, after talking about the rock on every trip, Ty said to his driving buddy, "You know what? I'd like to guess how much that rock weighs. In fact, I'd bet a thousand I can come closer than you."

The guy had a little gamble in him, so he answered, "Well, we might just get that on for $1,000."

"All right," Ty said. "Tomorrow when we pass by here we'll stop and go out there and guess at the weight of it." And they drove on to the poker game.

The next day they pulled the car off the side of the road and started looking at the rock. "You want me to guess first, or you wanna guess first?" Ty asked.

"Don't make no difference," the guy answered. "I'll guess first if you want me to."

He guessed how much the rock weighed and they wrote his number on a slip of paper. Then Ty walked around the rock, studied it, kicked it with his boot, got off to the side a little distance and looked it over again, all that bull. Finally he made his guess and wrote it down next to the other guy's. "You know, I've always been a good guesser of weights, how much anybody weighs or their height or whatever," Ty said, putting down his story. "You know what? I bet I won't miss the weight of that rock within a hundred pounds."

"You're crazy," the guy said. "Ain't no way you can guess it that close, Ty."

"Well, I'll bet another two thousand that I can."

"I believe I'll just call that bet," the guy answered, figuring he had the nuts.

"How are we gonna find out what the rock actually weighs?" Ty asked him.

"We can find somebody in town with a winch truck to weigh it for us," the unsuspecting fella suggested, and with that, they drove back to town.

Ty had given the man with the truck $100 or so in advance not to say anything about it when they got there. When they drove into his filling station, Ty asked, "Who runs this place?"

"I do," the man answered.

"Well, we've got a bet on about the weight of a rock out in the desert," Ty said. "Is it possible for you to drive outside of town with your truck, load it with your winch and bring it back here so that we can weigh it?"

"Yeah, I probably could, but it'll cost you about $100."

"That's all right. The winner will pay you."

So they went through the process of loading up the rock, bringing it back downtown, weighing it and returning it to its resting place by the side of the road. Ty missed its weight by 75 pounds, won $3,000 on the bet. As always, anytime it looked like you had the nuts [the advantage] on Ty, you didn't.[44]

There are two things to be learned from these stories. The first is that when someone claims he can do the impossible and wants to bet on it, take it as a given that he can do it.

When I was a young branch manager in Manhattan, I hired a smooth-talking salesman. One evening after work, he bet everyone in the office he could drink three eight-ounce glasses of beer in five seconds. To make a long story short, after everyone laid out their money, he lined up the three glasses, threw one glass down his gullet after another and finished the job in about three seconds. (Soon after, I found him working for another company at the same time he was working for me, and I fired him. I guess he could not resist being slick.)

The second point to these stories and how they all relate to "Rule 1" is that while they may seem funny, they are not. If life were just about the living of it and not about improving yourself, then you might say Titanic Thompson had a full and entertaining one—despite the fact that he hustled many, shot a few along the way, and died penniless and alone in a nursing home. But life is about much more than just the simple living of it, and so being dishonest must be seen for what it is: an action that wounds the mind and thereby cheats the cheater.

Everyone who uses their given or developed talents to take unfair advantage of others, even when successful at it, takes a hammer to the image of their own good natures. As such, self-respect is lost in every disrespectful action toward or judgment of others, its return possible only through extending respect, sharing it being the means by which you realize it belongs to you.

From the janitor to the chairman of the board, each person in the organization is part of the whole, equal in worth and rights, deserving of the same feelings of appreciation and inclusion as you. If you believe that others have needs, wants, and rights less important than your own, you will, like Titanic Thompson and every other slickster who slithers through the halls of business preying on the unwary, be lost in dreams of self-aggrandizement, with nothing to look forward to but the fear of being alone, with no one left to rob and nothing left to do.

The Price of Lunch

Rule 2: Everyone is untrustworthy, and therefore no one deserves trust.

One of the first business transactions in America took place in 1626 when Peter Minuit of the Dutch West India Trading Company "purchased" Manhattan Island from the Manhattan Indians for twenty-four dollars' worth of merchandise. Not long after, another trading company began to take unfair advantage, this time of a nation. From *Blue Blood* by Edward Conlon:

> Although heroin and cocaine are so contagious that they sell themselves, major epidemics of drug abuse have always been sponsored by organizations of extraordinary dedication and ruthlessness. Long before the Mafia, the Colombian cartels, and the Burmese warlords there was the British East India Company, against which the first war on drugs was lost.
>
> In the two opium wars of the mid-19th century, the Chinese fought the British to prevent them from smuggling opium into China, which they had done since the late 1700s to improve the balance of trade. Though there were other issues behind the conflict, the bald fact of the matter is that the British created the largest intentional outbreak of a disease in human history. One-third of the Chinese were regular users, and half of those were 'sots'—hopeless, useless and nearly lifeless. The Chinese were forced to cede Hong Kong after the first war in 1842, and to legalize the drug after the second in 1860.[45]

Obviously, though, reasons for mistrust did not begin with the trading companies, or with the Dutch or British. From the time of Paris abducting Helen, through that of Rebekah and Jacob cheating Esau of his birthright, on through the Inquisition, slavery, the Holocaust, the Bataan Death March, stolen elections, Enron, and the like, examples of cruelty toward others are varied and legion, creating the image of a social climate that seems to come down to "eat or be eaten." This kind of cruelty and mistrust isn't limited to history, either. Simply watch the evening news, follow a political campaign, read letters to the editor, scan the talk shows, or see what happens if you do not pay the credit card bill on time. On this surface level, devour or be devoured appears to be the truth of the world.

However, just because duplicity and murderousness have been the companions of man since we can remember, this does not prove that they are inherent and ineradicable. Think of it this way: if you have at times fallen and become untrustworthy, as we all have, does that mean you will never be trustworthy again? Absolutely not.

But if you disagree with me—that is, if you believe that because of your mistakes you will never be able to trust yourself with anything—then surely you will find no reason to trust anyone else, and this kind of universal mistrust of others is a hefty personal price to pay. If you can bear to face this very important dilemma, however, you may realize that you can escape your untrustworthiness. How? By recognizing that being deceitful and untrustworthy serves no useful purpose and, in fact, will only cost you—not to mention those around you. Let me give you an example. When I was about seventeen, an opportunity came along for some friends and me to buy an inexpensive car. Four of us chipped in to purchase it. I was thrilled, not so much because of the car, an old heap of a stick shift, but because at last I could learn to drive. The others, all being a year or two older than me, already knew how. For some reason, however, when it came time to register the car, I was not around, so the others went to the motor vehicles bureau without me. When they returned, I was surprised and disturbed to learn what they had done: to avoid having their parents be considered the ones responsible for the car, they had it registered in my father's name.

My next logical step would have been to say, "You can't do that," and then to rip up the registration. But at that stage in my development, I was neither logical nor trustworthy. I wanted only what I thought that car would offer me: the chance to learn to drive, transportation where few had any, fun in painting it a bunch of different colors and driving it around the neighborhood, and the ability to impress other kids and maybe even girls.

So I compromised my principles, which were a paltry few at the time anyway, and agreed to let the matter stand—but on two conditions. First, I would be the primary owner and, thus, the one who kept it most of the time. Second, the most experienced driver would teach me how to drive: a decent, personable guy who later became a drug dealer and, after a problem, was eliminated, disappearing and never to be heard from again.

Now the reason I was so untrustworthy in the matter was not because I didn't respect my father and my obligation to be faithful to him. I was pretty well past my stint of rebellion against my parents, and regardless, even with his name on the registration, it had little to do with him. On the contrary, I did what I so shamefully did because I didn't respect myself. I let my lust for the car and for the benefits I believed it would bring me replace my good sense and my responsibility to my father and myself alike. I broke the bonds of filial piety and put my personal interests in front of my shared interests with my dad. The "reward" for this was that, despite the fact no harm was done (I had no accidents and he never found out about the registration), I felt terrible about my lapse in integrity for a long time afterward.

For me, one of the important discoveries to come out of that matter and other situations like it was the recognition that, in reality, it is *never* the other person I attack first when I am untrustworthy, but *always* myself. Stated simply, by not respecting my father's rights and not putting my desires in their proper secondary place, I labeled myself unworthy of trust.

Years after this event, while living in California, I was visited by a few old friends from New York, including the fellow who had put my father's name on the registration. I had not seen or spoken to him in well over twenty years, but within the first few minutes he was in my home, he pulled me aside and said, "Hey, I want to apologize for what I did with your father's name on the car registration. It was a lousy trick and I'm sorry for it." For all these years, both he and I felt bad over our individual self-betrayals—a prime example of how no one emerges as a winner in such situations.

Acting without honor always boils down to this: *psychologically speaking, "there ain't no free lunch."*

Accepting Yourself as a Learner

Rule 3: I already know how I should think and respond.

If you are convinced that your experiences have taught you what everything means in life and therefore shown you how to respond to it all, you have closed your mind to learning anything new. Yet learning must go on all the time if you are to avoid stagnation.

To some, learning from everything may sound like an unwanted assignment. To others, to be told they can learn their way out of limitation is the greatest news of their lives. Once I define the parameters of my education as ending with formal training, I restrict what should be an ongoing process. Saying I have little more to learn is the defense of my laziness and the ignorance it masks, an attitude that serves only to retard my potential.

At work, what are the requirements for growth other than renouncing the false safe haven of ignorance? Not much. The way to grow tall and sturdy is not that complicated: to put forth a decent effort, to learn from your mistakes, and to continue doing your best to improve. Don't let yourself be tempted into believing it can't be that simple, because it is.

Think about it. What else could the answer be? It cannot be that you should be doing better than you are. That's just unkindness speaking. Every hateful thought you become aware of that claims you should be doing better than you are right now is a statement without meaning or sense. Why? Because it says you are *not* doing your best now, which cannot be. You *are* doing your best right now, even if it is not your best in terms of your potential. This also means that even when you were at your most careless, you were doing the best you could, at that moment.

What do I mean? When someone acts inappropriately, it comes from being lost in a cloud of ignorance regarding the consequences of their actions. If those who act inappropriately understood that their negative actions would always "return" to hurt them, they would discontinue what they were doing. It comes down to this: If people don't understand, they don't understand, and no one who does understand ever demands that those who don't should before they can. The only other possibility, other than ignorance, is that those who misbehave are masochists, and if they are masochists, they are quite obviously unbalanced. Therefore those who unconsciously or consciously do wrong, which is certain to bring them pain later, are either ignorant or insane. And the knowing and the sane, seeing this, find no reason to condemn them, and so they don't. As Socrates said in Plato's *Protagoras*: "When people make a wrong choice … the cause of their mistake is a lack of knowledge…. To act beneath oneself is the result of pure ignorance."[46] In this light, even your greatest blunders can be seen for what they were: errors you made while stumbling about in the darkness of a lack of proper information.

A good example of my learning from an error I made at work is as follows. Early on in my business-equipment career, I made a big sale of billing machines to the Manhattan offices of a large French cosmetics company. The system I sold was married to a large bank of NCR (National Cash Register) machines. After the installation I walked out the door of the account feeling well-satisfied with myself and soon after cashed my largest commission check to that date. To keep the story short, the installation ran into difficulties. That's when an older and more experienced NCR salesman named Joe stepped in and convinced the customer, as he should have in his position as a competitor, that the problem lay in our equipment and not in the joint system. Before I knew what was happening, our equipment was out and more of his was in. Forever after, I was unable to regain the position of trust I had established with the client; my commission statement showed a huge deficit, which I was obligated to repay; and I was, to put it mildly, more than mildly upset.

I blamed the customer for not giving me an adequate chance to set things right. I blamed that back-stabbing so-and-so of an NCR salesman for setting me up. I blamed the installation team for not doing a better job. In general, I blamed life, bad luck, and virtually anything else I could think of. But then, thankfully, in relatively short order, I came to my senses and accepted the truth: *I* was the salesman on the account and therefore the responsible party, and if I wanted to hold someone accountable, it would have to be me. So I did. I accepted that I had screwed up and that it was my own mistake that had cost me so much money, which was an especially bitter realization at the time because I had so little. The next thing I did was determine that I would *never* put myself in that position again, that I would never let a sale slip away by being careless.

The point of all this? I learned something valuable from my mistake. From that day forward, I paid much closer attention to my accounts and installations, and I never lost another sale for such a controllable reason. Therefore, even though I initially lost, I gained over the long term.

What more do you need to learn to find your own way out of the state of ignorance? Just a few short statements. Discover the value in saying, either to yourself or to another, those four great words: "I do not understand." (The fact is that unless you are already among the few and the wise, you do not understand.) In many cases, "I'm not sure" and "I don't know, but I will find out and get back to you" are also worthy external responses, signs of the self-confidence that allows you to tell the truth. But the greatest words of all to say to yourself are "I don't understand, and that's okay."

What we want to do is accept ourselves as what we are, people who have much to learn, laying down the burden of pretending to be masters before our time, aware we need the help of present wisdom in our every undertaking, grateful to be assured it is still our good friend.

The Only Worthy Goal

Rule 4: There are substitutes for tranquility.

Since tranquility—or peace of mind—is the proof of contentment, can it have a substitute? Can anything this valuable ever be replaced by something less worthy; for example, the fleeting "benefits" offered by one of the following five?

1. *Excitement.* Excitement is not the wondrous thing it presents itself as. In truth, excitement is nothing more than a deceptive form of fear. Getting excited is like getting high, each time resulting in an adrenaline depletion and a consequential hangover-like depression. In that way, seen rightly excitement is closer to an enemy than an ally. And above all stay on guard against excitement's most extreme form: euphoria. Because the higher you go, the greater the subsequent fall.

2. *Pleasure.* The ancient Greeks believed in the idea of "all things in moderation," not because they were self-sacrificing, but because they understood the value of balance and therefore were wise. Yet there is clearly nothing wrong with enjoying oneself, and anyone who thinks there is not only is not making sense, but is usually expressing an uncertainty about the judgment of the Almighty.

Once, when Kathy and I were in New York at Christmastime, my mother asked us to accompany her to Midnight Mass, and the three of us attended the service, which was quite nice. About a week later, I was back in California on the phone with my mother—who was always trying to figure out how to get me back to the church—when she asked me another one of her loaded questions: "What did you think of Midnight Mass?" Because we had found it pleasant, I said, truthfully, "We really enjoyed it." To this, my mother immediately responded, "Oh, you're not supposed to *enjoy* it."

I would imagine this response was the result of her belief and, perhaps, hope that after living the hard life she did, she could gain heaven through sacrifice and suffering, and that, as a result, at least in religious matters, the last thing you were supposed to do was have a good time while you went about them.

But as much as sacrifice and suffering, prolonged remorse, and walking on one's knees on painful pilgrimages add no value to a person's rewards, neither does pleasure. Real happiness comes from doing our utmost to do what is right in big matters and small, which is how "virtue is its own reward" steps off the page and comes to life. In comparison, pleasure should simply be seen as what it is—something that is pleasant until it is overly embraced. After that, pleasure is nothing more than an addiction, leaving you with a growing desire for more.

3. *Power.* The first of the dictionary's definitions for *power* is "possession of control, authority, or influence over others."[47] Should I accept this as a substitute for tranquility? Would anyone in his or her right mind? It is one thing to find myself in a position of power as a natural result of my good efforts, but it is quite another to chase desperately after it. Since the only power worthy of being sought after is the power to be helpful, because this alone is what benefits me or you, this should become the standard for seeking for all of us.

I was once driving around the Big Island of Hawaii with Kathy at my usual rate of speed when out of the blue, she said, "You don't understand."

"Understand what?" I replied.

"Understand the purpose of driving," she said.

"And what is the purpose of driving?" I responded.

"Why, the comfort of your passenger, of course," she said, smiling.

She was so right on and so clever about the way she said what was, in effect, "Hey, slow down, you're making me dizzy," that I started laughing, immediately reduced my speed, and, to the best of my ability, never forgot about what she said whenever I drove her or others.

This, along with many other lessons in awareness, caused me to consider more carefully the purpose of everything, leading me to the conclusion that the purpose of living could be summed up in a similar way: "The comfort of others." And while I am well aware how difficult it is to embrace such an idea, I see reason to try to keep in mind that it is the worthiest goal.

Power over others in itself counts for nothing. Power over the ambition for power counts a lot. Simply put: unless the power I gain brings with it the equanimity I will need to meet life's unpredictable challenges adequately, it cannot possibly have value over tranquility.

4. *Fame.* Give me a break. Do I really want reasons to support the uncertainty bred by my notions of self-importance?

5. *Money.* Many believe that money can buy happiness, or at least an exit from misery, but I now know better. Just as those who move to beautiful California to escape their problems find to their dismay that their troubled minds, the real source of their distress, have moved there with them, so it is with the ones who pin all their hopes on money only to discover it is really a neutral factor in determining contentment. Money is neither bad nor good; simply what you make of it.

To live within the confines of the Four Rules of Confusion is to sentence yourself to waking up, when you are old and gray, to the disappointing realization that you have spent your life going nowhere. Therefore, if you are to avoid ending up in this shameful condition, now is the time to begin your escape from emotional swings over nothing to the peace that comes only with balance. In the final analysis, *there is no substitute for tranquility.*

12

Balance

They're Coming for You

Do we live in a logical and balanced or an illogical and unbalanced society? Many years ago my first wife's mother, who was from New York, became quite ill while vacationing at our home in California. She was hospitalized, diagnosed with pancreatic cancer, and told she had only a short time to live. She was so sick she couldn't eat normally, so the doctors put a feeding tube in her stomach. In the evenings after work, I would go to the hospital and, through that tube, feed her liquids the hospital provided. One evening while we were engaged in this process, she began to hemorrhage badly, blood spewing out of her mouth and nostrils. I pressed the emergency button, and the nurses and doctors came running. They rushed her into the operating room, and with an extraordinary effort and a number of transfusions, saved her life.

Later, after additional time in the hospital, she got well enough to return to New York, where she was hospitalized again. A few weeks later, my wife and I went to visit her and found her deeply jaundiced and in a coma, her legs twitching uncontrollably. Days later, she died.

Was that a fitting end for a hard-working and decent woman? Or, since she had an incurable disease, should she have been allowed to exit quickly when she hemorrhaged? Was "saving" her for nothing more than further pain—as society demands—anything other than disguised cruelty?

Are we balanced or are we unbalanced? Kathy and I had four pets, among them, two cats who lived for many years. When the two cats neared their end, they, at different times, became pretty sick. Once the veterinarian assured us they were not going to improve, our first thought was to figure out how to alleviate their distress. In both cases, because they were suffering and were not going to get better, we chose to have them put to sleep. We went to the vet, held them gently as they received a painless injection, and kept hold on them as they died peacefully in a matter of seconds. To me, that was balanced because it was kind.

Is the way we conduct our affairs balanced? When the company I headed up was about to go public, we did what were called roadshows, which consisted of giving presentations in multiple cities to groups of institutional investors, bankers, insurance companies, and the like. On one such trip, I gave in one day an early-morning breakfast presentation in New York, a mid-morning presentation in Boston, a late-lunch presentation in Philadelphia, and a dinner presentation in Tampa, and then later spent the night in Miami. For another roadshow, I found myself traveling to twenty different cities in Europe and the U.S. in less than two weeks. Then, a couple of days later I went to Tokyo for a day. Such traveling may have been necessary because of the way the system was, but it surely wasn't logical or balanced.

Do we take a balanced approach to life? Technological progress allegedly will lead to our being able to live up to an average of 120 years. But who, besides those afraid of the wonders of dying, would want to? There isn't enough room on the planet as it is.

Doesn't it seem greedy to want to hang around, taking up space and resources that should naturally go to the young?

What is balanced action? Is it beneficial to society as a whole to automate a function that ends up costing a skilled worker his or her job simply because it is more efficient for the company? Isn't the skilled, tax-paying worker an integral part of society? Are those who have taken over the world of business and become, at least in their own minds, the new upper crust actually helping all of us, themselves included, to live a better life? Do you ever pause in your daily doings long enough to wonder why drug prices and college tuitions and the like consistently outpace inflation, and often by a wide margin? Can you see that because the middlemen screwed the poor so tightly to the ground that there was little room to screw them further, they have, and with a vengeance, turned on the middle class, working their way as rapidly as possible toward *you*? When that day arrives, will you feel such tactics are reasonable?

In the May 7, 2007, issue of *Forbes Magazine,* the publisher, Steve Forbes, says:

> There are plenty of bad ideas circulating that could create the conditions for destructive political and economic policies.... Inflation [mainly in higher commodity prices like oil] has also prompted a massive amount of borrowing [by today's "middlemen"] for corporate takeovers and stock buybacks. The borrowing binge will enrich investors in the short term. But longer term it's setting up a train wreck that could be even more destructive than the gaudy bursting of the high tech bubble in 2000.[48]

Does that sound balanced?

In *Conde Nast Portfolio Magazine*'s premier issue, Tom Wolfe, author of *The Bonfire of the Vanities*—a bestseller about the financial "Masters of the Universe," the middlemen of twenty years ago—writes about finding some of today's ilk "even coarser buccaneers than their predecessors could have imagined being," a number of them making $500 million to $1 billion in one year. In the following excerpt from the article, Wolfe amusingly juxtaposes an exclusive, older country club with one young billionaire's new house:

> Imagine how it [the old country club] would look if it were set beside Stevie Cohen's own 32,000 square foot clubhouse [his home] and 14 acres of grounds! Next to Stevie's art collection—which is nothing less than a world-class museum!—Stevie's indoor basketball court, year-round swimming pool under glass, his gym, his spa facility, his theater for movies and every other electronic medium, his hair salon, two putting greens complete with sand traps and a fairway in between, and, as the pièce de résistance, an ice rink the size of Rockefeller Center with a 30' by 40' rink house for the Zamboni [the large machine that cleans and conditions the ice].[49]

Does that sound balanced?

Finally, speaking of the attempted retaliation of those middlemen "wanting nothing so much as to replicate the status symbols and customs of old money," and unable to gain admission to the old-line clubs in New York, Wolfe says:

> So in the spring of 2005, they opened their own club, the Core Club, in midtown Manhattan, a club to beat all clubs, a billionaire's club. No amenity would be regarded as too over-the-top. Every member working out in the club's fitness center would have a butler at his elbow.... [T]he prospects of the ultimate club seemed so swell, 100 people ponied up $100,000 each as "elite founding members"... [and] each of the other 400 members agreed to pay an initiation fee of $55,000

… plus $1,000 a month in dues…. [T]he club remains flush with cash and Croesuses. Some have been saying, however, that there are reports that the members are not exactly wild about going to the club to beat all clubs anymore.

If so, the reason is not hard to find. At the Soho House, and wherever else the younger smart set convenes, the Core Club is now known as the club for people who can't get into clubs.

And on and on stagger those caught in the unbalanced chase after nothing other than wealth and power.

Surmounting Fate

As surprising as it may sound, the effective way out of imbalance is not through changing your behavior to make it more "appropriate." Why? Because, while it always makes sense to act appropriately, doing so without bringing your thinking in line with your behavior will only result in a further state of imbalance; the thinking, in effect, will conflict with the behavior. So while dealing with negative opinions through positive thinking and polite behaviors—for example, pretending you're not upset when you are—can be a helpful start, it will never reduce your state of personal imbalance. As Kenneth Wapnick puts it, you do not eliminate dirt by sweeping it under the rug, and if you continually do so, after a while you have a very uneven surface to walk on.[50]

The real answer to balance, then, is in becoming continually honest with yourself about how you are feeling and what you are thinking right now. To learn to do this, you must recognize how little you know about yourself; something few, especially the more "successful" among us, find easy to accomplish. As a dormant muscle feels strain when it is first brought back into use, so a mind comfortable in what it "knows" feels stress when it must start stretching again to accommodate new thought.

Likely, you understand how, just as a closed hand cannot accept anything given to it, a belief system closed in upon itself learns nothing new. What may not be as apparent, however, is that the closed mind not only loses whatever the new ideas offer, but also deprives itself of the benefits that come from reconsidering old, dysfunctional beliefs. Such insular reasoning is not only suffocating, unbalanced, and defended by a false sense of certainty; it also, more importantly, limits your development.

The "already knowing" people who partake in such supposed reasoning usually function quite mechanically, spending little of their time at work learning about themselves and most of their free time in sleep, distraction, bragging, and worry. Only when they accept themselves as being worthy of close attention can they find the energy to demand that their attention awaken from its nap. It is at this point that they can find the motivation to take on the challenge of introspection and the rigor of undoing all their minds' less-than-productive notions. That's not to say the process will be any less challenging or rigorous, however. So if you find such growth attractive and decide it is for you, please realize that it will not be a short-term, quick-fix, let's-accomplish-this-real-soon undertaking.

Why? Due to our deeply rooted identification with our often mistaken but still cherished beliefs, it takes time, patience, and fortitude to unglue and release our attachment to them. If you can picture the cramped crookedness of your wrong-mindedness as a corkscrew long imbedded in a dense mahogany tree, you will realize the answer is not to rip it from its place, but to reverse the position it has become so accustomed to slowly. In real life, that means not fighting against your slanderous notions, but just watching them carefully, staying with their spitefulness until they, of their own ephemeral nature, disappear. It means sticking with it every time you fall into the frustration engendered by believing the noisy complaints of wrong-mindedness that try to dissuade you from pursuing your purpose, and, instead, patiently awaiting reason quietly to say, "Look, friend, everyone has to be somewhere.

Is mowing the lawn or washing the car or taking the dog for a walk all that different from working on the problem at hand, even if it is one that vexes and befuddles you? Is this issue you are dealing with really overwhelming, or is it only your attitude that makes it seem so? Is your equilibrium gone forever, or have you merely misplaced it?"

Over time, your ability to maintain your sense of purpose will be strengthened by the diminution of respect you offer to each passing hardship, and you will begin to look down on and not up to what seemed so frightening before. As Camus so aptly said in *The Myth of Sisyphus*, "There is no fate that cannot be surmounted by scorn."[51]

If you keep Camus's idea in mind each time the towering sea of emotion threatens to engulf you, you will be heading toward the acceptance that you can conquer not only this particular problem, whatever it may be, but every one that follows. Your weakest beliefs and all their shuddering expressions may claim that you cannot, but deep within, you will know that they are lying, and that you *will* return to home port: the middle of the center of the state of perfect balance.

This process—and not becoming a "Master of the Universe"—is how to undo anxiety, how to learn to function from the quiet center within and be at peace with whatever you do.

The Train of Hatred

Along my way I have often been out of balance, making many mistakes, some small, some huge. At times I have been deceived by my stupidity, forgotten my sanity, believed I was badly treated, and then acted as mean as mean can be. I have slandered people and I have been slandered. I have judged people and I have been judged. I have cheated people and I have been cheated. I have lived an obedient life, a fervent life, a wild life, a successful life, a studious life, and a reasoning life. And I have tried to think deeply about everything I have experienced along my way. What conclusion have I come to? Hatred is a powerful force in the unguarded, unbalanced mind. That is why it is far easier to hurt another than not to, especially when you have deluded yourself into the conviction that you are justified in doing so.

For this reason, perhaps the hardest lesson you will face on your way to achieving balance will be on how to disregard the urge to respond to violence with violence, to stand aside from the calls to war that plague our minds. I know from long experience just how difficult it can be to hold one's tongue in the face of hostility, especially with the viciousness of wrong-mindedness so fiercely demanding that you respond to the other's mistakes in kind.

There is an old story that relates to this: Above a little mountain town there lived a very wise man. One day a young woman in the village below, under pressure from her parents to name the father of the child she had just borne, blamed the wise man for her plight. The parents and the townsfolk were furious to think of how she had been misused, and as a group they marched up the hill and pounded on the wise man's door. When he answered, they thrust the child on him, saying, "Here, you evil-doer, take responsibility for what you have done." The wise man, understanding the situation for what it was, accepted the child from the townspeople, replying simply, "I see."

About two years passed, during which time the young woman's remorse grew and grew until one day when she could stand the pain of false accusation no longer, she finally confessed to her foul deed, identifying the young man next door as the real father of the child. When the parents told their neighbors what had happened, they all felt terrible about what they had done. So they marched again as a group up the hill to the wise man's house, knocked on the door, and sincerely apologized, asking for the child back. To which the wise man, as he handed over the child, replied only, "I see."

This story demonstrates that true success is not about gaining or being right. Instead it is about meeting the next issue you face, the next mistake you make, the next memory of your mistake, or the next memory of the mistake of another that presents itself to your awareness, without resistance; meeting them all with the quiet response of "I see." And while that state of balance may not be today's reality for you, it certainly can be today's goal.

An important part of finding your way back to this ultimately rational condition is in becoming willing to apologize when you make a mistake. Apology is an important aspect of the innate power that resides in everyone. Used sincerely, it is helpful in bringing order to your psychological home. Conversely, used insincerely or left unused, it increases the turmoil you experience.

In an angry situation, however, reaching that rational state of mind that allows you to apologize can sometimes be difficult. When I was young, for a period of time, I was both willful and stubborn. Fortunately for my longer-term well-being, my father was, too. We had such enormous difficulties with each other that at one point, while living in that tiny apartment, we both decided the best way to handle our substantial differences of opinion about everything was by ceasing to speak to each other.

For six weeks, day and night, we passed each other in those cramped quarters without uttering a sound. Finally, my mother came to me and said, "You're going to have to speak to your father."

I immediately replied in youthful pomposity, "I am not going to speak to him. He is the man and I am the boy. Let him speak to me."

"You are going to have to speak to him first," she said.

Again, I responded willfully, "I will not go to him first. He is the father and I am the son."

And again, my mother insisted.

Somehow, shortly thereafter, I found the appropriate graciousness to go to my father. And when I did, when I put out my hand and said, "I'm sorry," to my astonishment, I found his hand already there, in forgiveness and friendship; he just had not extended it until then.

The idea behind this is that while sincere apology may not always make the mistake disappear, it will always make the mental disturbance disappear, and as such, must be stronger than both judgment and anger. Therefore we should exercise it more often, to strengthen not it, but our conviction of its power.

Of course, to say that we should learn to apologize more often implies that we expect ourselves to continue to make mistakes. So? For those who choose to learn continually, the world becomes a school. In this school, the painful consequences of our errors are actually valuable; they remind us not to continue in their paths. This is one of the ways mistakes become our teachers: feeling badly about them afterward motivates us not to repeat them.

Facing the attraction of accusation and finding balance in such hostile, frictional situations boils down to this: when I am ready to be honest with myself, I will see that my attempt to drag the other person through the sewer of my hate and suffering is actually just a way to conceal my condemnation of myself for my own mistakes and similar actions.

No one who is in his right (in other words, rational) mind condemns another, even if the other is in his wrong mind. Ergo, when I find myself condemning another, I must be in my wrong mind, otherwise there would be no hatred—disagreement, perhaps, but never personal condemnation. The resolution to this condition, then, is to forget about what the other is doing and find my way back to my own right mind.

When required, apology is a step in this direction. Yet apology, to be sincere, must be married to forgiveness. Not forgiveness of the other for what he is doing, but for what he is *not* doing, which is forcing me into my miserable state of wrong-mindedness. And, along with that, forgiveness of myself for having chosen to be in that state in the first place.

In summary, the effective approach to the mendaciousness of hostility is this: *When the train of hatred comes whistling through the corridors of your mind, try to offer it no resistance, all the while remembering this is a defense against the truth.* Do not deny it, do not oppose it, do not believe its arguments, and do not give it the power to cause you to speak or act. Just watch it until it disappears. If you dedicate yourself to this proposition, you will no longer see the external as the source of what you experience within. As a result, your inner hatred will seem less and less fearsome each time it comes barreling round the bend—because watching it, without acting on or believing in its counterproductive advice, always makes it shrivel, shrink, and fade away.

13
Know Thyself

Everyone Is Searching

In his book *Listening with the Third Ear,* Theodor Reik, a psychoanalyst and one of Freud's earliest students, makes this case for deeper sensitivity:

> In addition to our conscious sense perceptions, we receive communications through other organs of perception which we cannot consciously call our own, although they are within us. We can treat these signals like any others. We can attend to them or neglect them, listen to them or miss them, see them or overlook them.
>
> Many of the gaps and errors in our psychological comprehension must be attributed to our inattention to these unconscious signals.... They ... supplement conscious perception. In certain cases they alone enable us to discern its significance or correct the significance we mistakenly ascribe to it.[52]

In other words, when we are not sensitive and alert, we are reacting to an incomplete picture. In such a condition, we are operating in the dark, which means we cannot expect to avoid bumping into things, or sometimes even stumble and fall. Yet, if we heighten our awareness and pay attention to everything, most importantly to ourselves, our comprehension and therefore our ability to think logically will improve and, along with that, our potential for success.

This means that for most of us there is much yet to understand, but that is good, for if the superficial things we saw every day were all of it, life would be a dull, cruel, and dismal affair indeed. Universally, the wise men of both ancient and modern times say that to attain such heightened awareness, you must first and foremost "know thyself."

Yet here is where it gets a bit tricky. Why? Because "know thyself" means different things to different people. After a reasonable consideration, you will see that it cannot mean to know the character you have made up to contend for your interests in the contest of business, but first to learn what you are underneath that character right now. No matter your present beliefs about advancement, you are not on a quest to improve the image you have developed, only to dissolve what you find disagreeable within it. Yet even that is tricky, because if you "do" something to dissolve it, you will add another layer to it, and that, in turn, will defeat your purpose.

This leaves you with the task, simple to state but difficult to accomplish, of achieving a crystal clear, nonjudgmental observation of yourself as you are at present: not the character you have developed, but the thinking going on underneath it. After all, if honesty is the only effective starting point, how better to begin your search for the truth of what you are than with an objective assessment of the state of your mind as it is here and now.

All That Hides in Darkness

Watching yourself carefully will disclose how often your thinking is prone to grave errors, with much of what you believe is true and react to as a given, coming from what is incorrect yet hidden from sight. As a simple example of the confusion we can unknowingly harbor within ourselves, imagine the following scenario: You go to work wearing a white shirt. During the day, someone comes along and says, "I really hate that blue shirt you have on." Aware that you are wearing a white shirt, you look on him in wonderment and smile at his mistake. Soon after, another person comes along, and after a bit of conversation she states that she believes you are incompetent. Before you know it, you find yourself, outwardly or inwardly, depending on her power over you, reacting furiously to her, defending yourself and denouncing her and all her rotten opinions. Yet why? Are you upset because she is a terrible liar? An insulting boor who has somehow reached into your mind and hurt your feelings? Or could your reaction, in fact, be a cover, one that you have quickly raised so that you will not have to look at what she said and then, even more difficult, look beyond it to the very source of your defensiveness?

What do I mean? Think about it. Why would you have had any more of a reaction to her insulting comment than you did to the mistaken attack on the color of your shirt? Could your vigorous reaction not be a confirmation that somewhere within you, you believe she has spoken fairly and exposed you for what you fear you may be? So, in that vein, does your problem lie in what she said or in your secret belief she may have spoken truly? If the latter, then who is most in need of a change of mind about you—she or you?

Looking at it this way, ask yourself in the final analysis whether she is an enemy or just someone who came along to point out part of your belief system that is in need of repair. Likely, you will find the answer to this question is the latter option. If so, ask yourself whether this "unconscionable insult" is really a justification for war or just another opportunity to correct a slander that you have unknowingly held against yourself. Should you hate her for what she said or be grateful to her for helping you bring an error in your self-appraisal to the surface—that is, into your awareness?

Such a questioning and reasoning process is the way out of self-hatred. It brings to your awareness, and then allows you to leave behind, all that hid in darkness, humiliating and bedeviling you.

In summary, then, vigilance, combined with an unmatched dedication to self-improvement, is the way out of the inclination to belittle yourself through the maladaptive means of defensiveness and blame. Without that, because the problem runs so deeply, you will forever remain the unruly pawn of your hidden beliefs, the put-upon servant of your vacillating emotions. This means that *nothing* is more vital to your well-being than a growing awareness of your mind's activities, along with a willingness to question what you were heretofore certain just had to be true.

The great sixteenth-century French essayist Montaigne said something about self-improvement well worth pondering. He said, "To compose our character is our duty ... to win, not battles ... but order and tranquility in our conduct. Our great and glorious masterpiece is to live appropriately. All other things, ruling, hoarding, building, are only little appendages and props, at most."[53]

14

Not Taking the Game Seriously

Mastering the Quick Exit

The idea discussed earlier, that perception is never objective, but, as Shakespeare said, is made so only by thinking, applies not only to how you see others but also to how they see you. Another's opinion of you is always subjective, coming from his self-formulated beliefs, filtered through and conditioned by his present state of mind. Even if you have just met someone, more often than not, his first impression of you is that you remind him of someone who looks or acts like you, and as such, he begins to fit you into the same mold as that other person. In addition, these impressions that we have of each other constantly shift and change; therefore, being inconstant, they are inaccurate and without merit.

Through this reasoning you can begin to harness your confusion, recognizing, for example—and this is an important example—that when a person assaults or applauds you, it has nothing to do with you *per se*, but only with whether he is finding his made-up and momentary version of you satisfying or not. This example is important because if you find yourself disappointed or pleased with his interpretation and response, you will react accordingly, unknowingly, and mistakenly, offering validity to his unstable and incorrect idea of you. Equally, if this is true it must also be true for you, not only in your variable opinion of him, but in your own changeable version of yourself. All this is proof positive that you do not know yourself, only this confused version of what you have identified with and, therefore, think you are. Yet can it be that you are not you, but rather some vacillating image, made up from what you like and dislike and have accepted as so from others and yourself?

Surely by now you understand that your business act is just an act. After all, you alone are the one who invented it, carefully sculpting the image you wished to present to the world, developing and overdeveloping certain aspects of your personality to further your career. This, too, is important, and you do not wish to be deceptive with yourself about it. You are not your persona. You are the one who constructed that persona, and it is no more you than your car, your computer, or your house is you. Accepting this as so means to see that being flattered or hurt are not what they appear, but rather the inevitable results of being captured by an emotional fantasy that says what happens to the image you hold of yourself actually happens to you.

In such a fantasy world, and a fantasy world it is, it will appear that concern, worry, excitement, and elation can and will be yours. Not one or two, but the whole mélange, one after the other in random order. This defines the problem, what you have done. You have agreed to participate fully in "the fair," entering willingly into the fantasy world of the game of business with the mistaken notion that you could figure out how to remain in the excitement and elation while paying minimal homage to the concern and worry that follow them. You have allowed yourself to become very partially engaged in a contest that you do not see is impartial, emotionally caught up in what is an impersonal game, such enslavement to events being the price of admission to its roller coaster world of constant ups and downs. Still, no matter how personally you may take it, business is never personal, and the character that you made up to play the game is not personal either, just a costume an actor puts on for his part in the play. It is not a bad thing or a good thing, just a costume for work. And what you make of it, and believe about it, and how you decide to use it is solely up to you.

If you do not perceive this, it is not because it is difficult to discern, but because you are afraid if you accepted it as so, the game might be less fun for you. Yet is the game as you play it now really that much fun? If the basic lot of the emotional "fan"—and when you take the game of business personally this is exactly what you have become, a fan of the player you made up—is concern, worry, excitement, and elation, and if never is how often you have been able to fend off concern and worry and get the excitement and the elation alone to stay, then the price for the positive is the acceptance of the negative and never anything less. This means, because the negative is so painful and the positive refuses to stay, you would be better served without either.

You may now see that these seemingly positive and always negative feelings are connected and cannot be separated, one following another as they pass through your life, delivering their cargoes of this time up and that time down, occasionally pausing before the next onslaught of excitement or depression. Is this continual imbalance something you really desire?

Is it fun to think that this miserable portion of reality is what you are to accept as your lot in life? And is it even reasonable to think that you should, without question, settle for this unnerving instability of being sometimes sad, sometimes happy, sometimes bored, and sometimes elated? Wouldn't it just be more sensible to refuse to remain in *any* of these insecure conditions?

Finally, for all who believe the thinking that says stability itself may turn out to be boring, or even depressing, I have news: complete peace is now offering a thirty-day guarantee. So if you reach tranquility and determine that you liked conflict better, peace will let you depart without charge or criticism. It will even provide you with a hand-stamp that lets you return when you are ready. In other words, what do you have to lose by giving it a try, except, perhaps, complacency?

If you can see what this offers, then it's time to start practicing the strategy of leaving both conflict and excitement the instant you become aware that you, once again, have been deceived by the trickery of your own subjective thought. Not to never be caught in such self-deception again—it will take a long time to get to that stage. But to take the necessary first step toward it by mastering the quick exit, learning to release yourself the moment you realize you have swallowed the bait, remembering that just underneath it there is always a hook.

Why Keep Score?

Consider the fable "The Snake" by writer Anne Herbert:

> In the beginning God didn't make just one or two people, he made a bunch of us. Because he wanted us to have a lot of fun and he said you can't really have fun unless there's a whole gang of you.[sic] So he put us in this playground park place called Eden and told us to enjoy ourselves.
>
> At first we did have fun just like he expected. We played all the time. We rolled down the hills, waded in the streams, climbed the trees, swung on the vines, ran in the meadows, frolicked in the woods, hid in the forest, and acted silly. We laughed a lot.
>
> Then one day this snake came along and told us that we weren't having real fun because we weren't keeping score. Back then, we didn't know what score was. When he explained it, we still couldn't see the fun. But he said that we should give an apple to the person who was best at playing and we'd never know who was best unless we kept score. We could all see the fun of that. We were all sure we were best.

It was different after that. We yelled a lot. We had to make up new scoring rules for most of the games we played. Other games, like frolicking, we stopped playing because they were too hard to score. By the time God found out about our new fun, we were spending about forty-five minutes a day in actual playing and the rest of the time working out the score. God was wroth about that. He said we couldn't use his garden anymore because we weren't having any fun. We said we were having lots of fun and we were. He shouldn't have got upset just because it wasn't exactly the kind of fun he had in mind.

He wouldn't listen. He kicked us out and said we couldn't come back until we stopped keeping score. To rub it in (to get our attention, he said), he told us we were all going to die anyway and our scores wouldn't mean anything.

He was wrong. My cumulative all-game score is now 16,548 and that means a lot to me. If I can raise it to 20,000 before I die I'll know I've accomplished something. Even if I can't my life has a great deal of meaning because I've taught my children to score high and they'll all be able to reach 20,000 or even 30,000 I know.

Really, it was life in Eden that didn't mean anything. Fun is great in its place, but without scoring there's no reason for it. God has a very superficial view of life and I'm glad my children are being raised away from his influence. We were lucky to get out. We're all very grateful to the snake.[54]

Like the misguided children in the fable, we all keep score. Some by money and special possessions, others by titles, power, or social status, and still others by the number of "friends" they collect. Some, literally, even by how terrifying they can be. There are those who are wrapped up in their intellects, looks, strength, or endurance, and others enthralled by their athletic ability or talent. Some are entranced with their own past episodes of valor; others appear humble while secretly fawning over their own religiosity. And a few actually believe they count for more than most due to the illustrious exploits, position, or wealth of their ancestors.

What all this fervent scorekeeping shows is that we have slipped into the sorrowful condition of taking ourselves far too seriously. We care what people say about us, worry whether we'll be invited to the next "important" function, and, without spending the necessary energy to arrive at the state of appreciating ourselves, are undeniably quite concerned about whether others like us or not.

In his well-known "Allegory of the Cave" (*Republic,* 7:514), Plato speaks of the uninformed and unwilling-to-be-taught prisoners of the cave who mistake illusion for truth and caprice for sense. In Plato's myth, the prisoners are "fettered from childhood" inside the cave in such a way that they can perceive only the wall before them. To their rear is the opening of the cave, and outside there is a fire "burning higher up and at a distance behind them, and between the fire and the prisoners and above them a road." Along the road, men walk, carrying things; some of the bearers remain silent, and some speak. The fettered prisoners, however, can perceive only the shadows cast by the passersby, thinking the shadows to be real objects. Likewise, the prisoners hear only echoes of the men's voices, mistaking them for real sounds. The prisoners talk to each other about the meaning of these sights and sounds. And the whole time they are caught in this world of illusion, they are firmly convinced they are dealing with reality.[55]

It is taking ourselves so seriously and business too personally that keeps us fettered to the meaningless, preventing our recognition of the meaningful. It keeps us believing that we understand, ignorant that we do not.

Everything Led Me Here

We all have different kinds of experiences at work and in the world. It's not what the experience was or is that matters though, only what you do with what it taught you afterward. Along my own way, I have found myself in the strangest of places. Running around at two in the morning with my footlocker over my head in military police school in Georgia. Spending the weekend with the owner of a mansion with a one hundred-foot living room in Hillsborough, California, discussing running part of a huge business takeover he was planning. Lying under the car that hit me the time I darted out into the streets in the Bronx, a neighborhood so welcoming that while the driver sat trembling at the wheel, someone threw a firecracker into her backseat.

Sleeping in a Salvation Army shelter in northern Florida as a runaway teenager; later, staying in places like the Queen's Suite at Claridges, the Reagan Suite at the Carlyle, and an ocean-front bungalow at the Mauna Lani. Taking the bus because I didn't have plane fare and pushing my car down the hill every morning to get it started; later, being chauffeured in cities around the world and flown here and there in jet helicopters and Gulfstreams. Wearing one cheap, coarse, heavy winter suit and fifty-cent ties every day for over a year in my junior salesman's position; later, and almost before I knew it, wearing hand-tailored Oxford suits and Hermès ties. Hungry enough to panhandle in Baltimore; later, handing out bills to every panhandler I met. Walking my sister's dog at 5:00 a.m., smiling as I realized that it was the hour I used to get home.

Shopping at Neiman Marcus and, in that same time frame, taking clothing and money to people living in shacks in Mexico. Having conversations with other would-be philosophers not many years after playing around with a killer because I was high and bored and wanted to. (I was with a couple of friends in a Mafia hangout in midtown Manhattan near where I worked and a notorious character, a hit man from the "Westies" named

"Harry the Hat," was on the other side of the crowded long and rounded bar. He was drunk and vehemently making a point to someone, causing the whole bar to go silent and shudder each time he loudly proclaimed, "I'm Harry the Hat." After about the fourth time he did this, into the ensuing silence I said, "No, *I'm* Harry the Hat." For a moment you could hear a pin drop, and then Harry, fortunately, burst out laughing and said, "Give the kid a drink.") Enjoying yearly horseback camping trips high in the Sierras with my three young sons and then watching all of them, nice boys one and all, struggle terribly, ruining their lives with alcohol and drugs. By myself with my one club—a five iron—at a deserted golf range in the middle of winter in New Jersey, hitting ball after ball in the cold, firmly resolved to teach myself how to play; years later, playing golf in Palm Springs with a small group that included the chairman of Merrill Lynch, the chairman of Arco, the commandant of the Marine Corps, and Ely Callaway.

Distinctly noting the first time I was able to afford a tuna-on-toast from a diner in my territory in Manhattan versus my usual brown-bag lunch; later, dining at the finest restaurants in New York, Paris, and London. Going out on Friday nights with three dollars to spend; later, making more money in a month than my hard-working father made in his lifetime. Scratching to get my foot in the door; later, turning down a highly paid CEO's position without a thought.

On and on my serial adventures came and went, and went and came. What did they all mean? Of themselves, absolutely nothing! This is the reason for my recounting them: to point them out as mere adventures, and then say that they, and all the many others high and low that I did not bother to mention, outside what they taught me about myself, were without any and all significance. I've met movie stars, intellectuals, political figures, highly placed executives, extremely wealthy people, religious leaders, boxers, ballplayers, golfers, gangsters, and what the world calls "big shots" galore, and the one thing they had in common was that they were all, for better or worse, merely human. Not only is no one person more or less important than another, equally, no experience is more or less important than another. Each has the potential to teach us something and is valuable only to the degree that we learn from it.

In the larger scope of that vast and silent universe that lies outside the constant and petty noise of the world and its supposedly wondrous, but actually, quite bloody history, my grandest moments and greatest blunders all fade into obscurity, leaving me with one thing alone, what I am right now. How else could it be? And how could any evanescent experience, long since passed and gone, add to or subtract from that simple fact? The purpose of *all* my adventures was singular: to aid in conveying me to here, and here of value only to the extent that I use those experiences to help me perceive properly now. Take it from me: I was a custodian's son from nowhere who became someone and went everywhere, only to find everywhere to be nowhere and himself to be nothing—without a proper perception.

15

The Cloak of Victimization

I'm Good Because You're Bad

As with most of us, it is likely there were periods in your life when it appeared that you were the prisoner of time and circumstance, unable to do much more than make the best of this "whatever," the latest in a long series of assaults on your peace and tranquility. At such times, it probably often seemed possible to escape only with the assistance of those heavy-handed "protectors," defensiveness and blame. They were the witnesses that proved you were a victim and therefore right, thereby the thought you might have been wrong was proven wrong. Yet was it? Do defensiveness and blame ever prove us right, or do they simply reinforce the notion of our wrongness? After all, if you knew you were not wrong, would you, even in the face of unfairness, find yourself with the need to prove yourself right?

Considering yourself maltreated always appears to contain a hidden "benefit" to you: to provide a secondary gain. What it seems to come down to is this: if you are the one being victimized, you cannot possibly be the victimizer; therefore, the other must be the bad guy and not you. You can see the products of this kind of thinking everywhere around you: at your place of work and in your personal life, as well as daily on the national and international stages.

Let me give you a brief example of my own past confusion about this and what I learned from it about the warped nature of my thinking. I was young and in a large, crowded local bar with a close friend. He was a wilder-than-most tough guy with a successful boxing career behind him in the paratroopers and, like a number of guys in the neighborhood, had a willingness to fight at any moment and for little reason. We had been drinking shots and beers in other neighborhood bars and were now shooting pool in this smoke-laden place filled with sixty or so half-drunk guys. Both good pool players, we were beating everyone and winning lots of money. And having had far too much to drink, we were making noise and generally acting up. The pool table was at the far end of a large room, and you had to walk down the long curved bar to get to it. And it was on just such a walk that my friend ended up in a fight with a guy named Little, who, ironically, was not.

As I heard the commotion and headed toward the action, a guy grabbed me around the arms and pulled me back, saying, "Stay out of it, Bob." Then, a friend of Little rushed through the crowd and came right up to me, and said, "Hey, you wanna go outside, Draper?" Being half-drunk, if not more so, and at the time a product of the Bronx and a captive of the idiotic "code" that dictated what a "man" must do in such circumstances, I replied without thought or hesitation, "Yeah," despite the fact the guy had thirty pounds and a couple of inches on me.

Now, even as well-lit as I was at the moment, I still knew this would likely be a losing proposition. So when we hit the doorway, I began to scuffle with him, trying in close-quarters fighting to equalize the situation. As this took place, he spun me around and I lost my footing, landing on the sidewalk outside the bar. As I started to get up, he caught me with a full boot to the head and down I went. As I began to get up again, he caught me with another fierce kick to the head. By this time a crowd was watching, and I could hear some of the guys yelling, "Stay down! Stay down!" But no, I was being a "man" and not having any of it. So I started up again and was rewarded for my bravado with another pretty severe kick to the face. On my fourth far-slower trip up (this was getting much harder to do), my buddy, having just finished with his fight inside the bar, leaped in to rescue me from further damage.

As I said earlier, I was neither big nor tough. Despite that, living where I lived, I had a number of fights, winning at least as many as I lost. It seemed like everybody who drank in that neighborhood got into fights. Some, like my friend, were exceptional at it. Yet, despite that (and this is an aside for every man who has ever questioned his courage or accused himself of cowardice) over the course of being with many tough guys and watching many fights and being in many violent and potentially violent situations, I discovered something interesting, that even the toughest, biggest, or meanest guys became frightened at times, and in that, backed down in one way or another. Not one was *always* brave.

Regardless, the point of my story has nothing to do with the fight, but only with what was going on in my mind. What happened? Strangely enough, on my third or fourth trip up off the concrete, I forget which, I experienced a rush of joy. Here I was, getting my head kicked in, and somehow, at the same time, I was feeling joyous. I couldn't understand it, but I was surely experiencing it. Even after a trip to the hospital for stitches, going back out for more drinking, suffering through a horrible hangover, and missing a week of work because I was all cut up (I told my boss, who came to see me, and everyone else at work that I had gone through a cab window in an accident), I still remembered that rush of joy. And because the feeling had been so strong, I found myself continuing to think about it. After a while, I concluded it must have come from my pride over "being a man" in difficult circumstances, as glorified by adventure books and movies and the code of the Bronx. Only much later did it dawn on me how wrong I was.

What I came to realize was that my rush of joy had nothing to do with being a man, nor anything to do with being a stand-up guy, a pretty silly concept anyway since I had spent the majority of the fight on the ground. What, then, was the source of this feeling? One thing. The sick idea of me being the innocent victim and the other person being the guilty victimizer. The event showed that I was "good" because it demonstrated so "clearly" that he was "bad."

This I learned is exactly what happens in every situation in which we appear, at least to ourselves, to be the victim of others or forces outside ourselves. We run around, protesting over and suffering under the burden of our physical or psychological pain, unknowingly relishing the fact that such things are happening, secretly defining them as proof that we are the ones who are "better than." This is a very effective, but quite harmful, defense against getting in touch with and undoing our hidden belief that the truth is we are "worse than."

16
Paying Attention

No Longer Wasting Time

A good example of a man who successfully resisted the lure of this inclination toward victimhood and found the power of his mind in the most exceptional circumstances was Vice Admiral James Stockdale. In a remarkable account, Admiral Stockdale, who was among other things a student of Epictetus, a college president, and a winner of the Congressional Medal of Honor, wrote about his life and his experiences in the Vietnam War.

During the conflict, he spent eight years as a prisoner of war, four in solitary confinement and two in leg irons, and was tortured fifteen times. To all of this, he responded, "So what? To live under the false pretense that you will forever have control of your station in life is to ride for a fall; you're asking for disappointment. So make sure in your heart of hearts, in your inner self, that you treat your station in life with *indifference*, not with contempt, only with *indifference*."[56]

After several years of abuse, he returned to his regular cell from "a couple of months in a tiny isolated cell we called Calcutta."

Soon after, he received a message of encouragement from his friend in the next cell, which he describes in this account:

"Back in my cell … I sat on my toilet bucket—where I could stealthily jettison the note if the peephole cover moved—and unfolded Hatcher's sheet of low-grade paper toweling on which, with a rat dropping, he had printed, without comment or signature, the last verse of Ernest Henley's poem 'Invictus.'

> It matters not how strait the gate,
> How charged with punishment the scroll,
> I am the master of my fate:
> I am the captain of my soul."[57]

The attitude called for in "Invictus" and exemplified by Admiral Stockdale and others like him is there not to be admired, but to be lived up to. Socrates faced an unjust death sentence with equanimity. Epictetus looked on his thoughts of maltreatment with contempt. James Stockdale responded to imprisonment and torture with an attitude that mirrored them both. These are not people with qualities that we don't possess; they are just people who refuse to continue to entertain doubts about themselves. So who is to say that you and I cannot learn to do the same?

In *The Handbook*, Epictetus is quoted as saying:

> How long do you put off thinking yourself worthy of the best things? What sort of teacher are you waiting for, that you put off improving yourself until he comes? If you delay paying attention to yourself, then without realizing it you will make no progress…. So decide now that you are a person worthy of making progress…. And if you meet with hardship … remember the contest is *now* … and do not put things off any longer…. Socrates became fully perfect in this way, by not paying attention to anything but his reason in everything he met with. You, even if you are not yet Socrates, ought to live as someone wanting to be Socrates.[58]

This makes great sense once we think of it this way: Assuming we are all born with the same capacity for reason and everyone has the same potential for developing that capacity, the greatness exhibited by Socrates, Epictetus, Stockdale, and the like is therefore something of which we are all capable. Yet how can we discover whether this is true unless we begin to do what we would naturally do if it were? What other way would there be to learn that we are—perhaps not in fact (yet), but certainly in potential—just like Socrates?

Here are a couple of others' thoughts about paying attention to our minds and setting aside self-doubt.

> *I wanted very much to be a person of value and I had to ask myself how this could be possible if there were not something like a [mind] that is in the life of a person and which could endure any misfortune or disfigurement and yet be no less for it. If one were to be a person of value that value could not be a condition subject to the hazards of fortune. It had to be a quality that could not change....*
>
> *I knew that courage came with less struggle for some than for others, but I believed that anyone who desired it could have it. That the desire was the thing itself. The thing itself. I could think of nothing else of which that was true.[59]*
>
> —Cormac McCarthy in *All the Pretty Horses*

> *As the mind governs the whole of our actions, everything will go to pieces unless it is working on the right lines. Set a thief to catch a thief, set the mind to watch the mind. It becomes in moments of excitement full of fancies, fears or useless wandering ideas.... [When this happens] then, in my experience, there is but one thing that can help, and that is to see the humor of the situation.*

If one is really amused at the absurdity of one's thoughts
and anticipations, he can respond by changing and coming
back to a more practical and firm outlook on things.[60]
—Joyce Wethered in *The American Golfer*

A frank assessment of our own thinking, especially when we are not calm, shows how often our distress and unrecognized desires lead us to wandering in an unsatisfying circle. This aimless journey usually begins with some sort of dissatisfaction, which stimulates effort that leads to accomplishment, which brings temporary satiation, which soon turns into a mental hunger and even despair, which cries out for help to alleviate its pangs, which allows thought to suggest that we form a new plan. This suggestion is what starts us over on the same senseless journey—only now it is disguised in a different form. Blindly going "forward" with such unrewarding striving is the "natural" result of living the unexamined life and the inevitable fate of the exceedingly ambitious: becoming perhaps champions in the arena and heroes to the unknowing, but not much more than people wasting time in the eyes of the wise.

Says Who?

In one sense remaining true to our deepest principles means going on like Dag Hammarskjold even when we "know not whither." This often means setting aside the seeming safety of just being a follower and recognizing, as Einstein put it, that "Unthinking respect for authority [without *or* within] is the greatest enemy of truth."[61]

In his statement it would appear that Einstein was alluding to the blind acceptance of Nazi dogma by otherwise reasonable German people. But, looked at carefully, the statement goes much further than that. It speaks to the problem of divisiveness (and its inbred conflicts) in our own blind acceptance of our "born into and therefore certain" beliefs about nationalism, religious tolerance, and what constitutes success in a world of almost infinite competition.

Life, examined and worth living, is a journey of learning that must include questioning what we have previously accepted if we are to continually shed our limitations. Friedrich Nietzsche aptly summed the idea up in one place in his classic *Thus Spoke Zarathustra*.

In brief, Nietzsche says that we need to first live in the world in a way that conforms to the basic rules of society, bearing our burdens, as we should at this beginning stage, like a camel, achieving our successes, experiencing our failures, obedient to the commands of the "great dragon" of authority he calls "Thou shalt." Here we function as loyal participants in the mundane contest, a place where many hope they have found safety and vainly attempt to remain in peace.

Yet this camel-like state, he proclaims, is only the first third of a three-part journey. The second leg of the journey is an inner one and begins when we refuse to continue to bow down like a camel and become more like a lion. This leg begins when we say, in what he defines elsewhere as the will to power, "Wait just a minute. I hear the calls to restriction, within and without, and all the demands for humble obedience, but because this unthinking conformity has produced such dissatisfying returns, I think I'll try to see if I can find my own way."[62] Thus the lion begins his part of the journey, challenging not only the values he had as a camel so readily accepted before, but the very source of his limitations. It is here, in the desert of what was once blind obedience, the lion stirs and begins to negate all he has been told that "insults his own soul," saying "thank you, but no thank you" to much of what he had said "yes, sir" to before.

After that, and only then, begins the third and final part of the journey, the part of the journey where, as Nietzsche puts it, the spirit "who has been lost to the world now conquers his own world."

Nietzsche calls us to join him as lions, asking us to respond to the inane "rules" that beleaguer us and the foolish practices that surround us with an attitude that meets their commands and persuasions with that wonderful question "Says who?"

17
Relating to Others

Violence and the Mind

Throughout history, using violence as the primary response to violence has led nowhere. Therefore, continuing in this fashion, which is exactly what we are doing, is akin to making regular deposits in a bankrupt bank. If we are prone to violence, and we hide that from ourselves by modifying our behavior and seeing ourselves as "helping" others, we may delude ourselves for a while, but we will accomplish nothing, inevitably returning to our violent ways.

Many have commented trenchantly on the general mess we are in and on that product of our decisions, this obscenely gruesome state called the "modern" world. Among them was President Dwight D. Eisenhower. He said, "Every gun that is made, every warship launched, every rocket fired signifies, in the final sense, a theft from those who hunger and are not fed, those who are cold and are not clothed. This world in arms is not spending money alone. It is spending the sweat of its laborers, the genius of its scientists, the hopes of its children.... This is not a way of life at all, in any true sense. Under the cloud of threatening war, it is humanity hanging from a cross of iron."[63]

Given this continuing phenomenon, what are you and I to do about what Matthew Arnold described as this "darkling plain … where ignorant armies clash by night"?[64] It cannot be that we should sit around wringing our hands in anguish over it, or that we should just hope and pray that it will disappear. So what are we to do? What else but to look within, face our misshapen thinking, recognize its viciousness, accept responsibility for it, and then change the source of our world: ourselves?

To look is to see and to see is the answer. The fact is that the arisals of madness surround us within and without; the additional fact being that we, like bleating lambs being led—strangely enough by ourselves—to the slaughter, continue to put up with it.

Defensiveness and Blame

If we are to escape the terrible consequences of our group insanity, we must first see that this is not just about those "others," but that we are prisoners too, and then come to understand what imprisons us. If we are often upset, and find such a contemptible state unacceptable, we can't find freedom through denial and pretending to be happy. Instead, we must face that it is so and learn why we fall prey to it. If being violent with or thinking hatefully of others makes us feel terrible later, and unbridled anger left unchecked, undealt with, and undisposed of, always does leave us with the same hangover psychologically that consuming too much alcohol does physically, then covering over such thinking and behavior with accusation and judgment is not an answer, just a defense against sanity.

In other words, if we are to find peace while the world about us, and even the thoughts within us, continue to whirl and rage, it is necessary we come to the complete acceptance of the part that we play in every emotional difficulty and, in that, recognize accusation for the defense of ignorance it is.

In speaking of this, Epictetus said: "It is the act of the ill-instructed man to blame others for his own bad condition, it is the act of one who has begun to be instructed to lay the blame on himself, and the act of one whose instruction is completed neither to blame another nor himself."[65]

Seeing the wisdom in Epictetus' statement should give us pause enough to ask ourselves, how well instructed are we? Honest answers to a few good questions might show us: Are we respectful of those in inferior positions? Are we generous? Do we understand the struggle everyone is going through and appreciate them for trying, even when their efforts seem substandard to our definitions of what is acceptable behavior? Do we see judgment as an expression of weakness, and tolerance the sign of strength? If not, simply put, we are still in need of self-examination.

In 1937, a movie called *Lost Horizon,* based on the novel of the same name by James Hilton, told the story of a group of people whose plane crashed in the Himalayas. After the crash, they broke through a snow-covered secret mountain pass into a land of harmony called Shangri-la. There they met a wise lama who told them the reason for living could be summed up in two words: be kind.

Is this suggestion of the lama a little too flighty for hard-driving, sophisticated "moderns" like us? A nice sentiment, perhaps, but hardly practical in the aggressive world we live in. Or, if we paused for a moment in our rush to nowhere to consider it carefully, might we see it as the only response that reasonable people could make, that is, once they saw the world as the caricature of responsibility toward all that it is and accepted that its belligerence came from their own lack of awareness, and therefore, without question, from no one but them?

"Ah, What Trouble?"

One of the themes of this book has been to speak of the strength and potential for decency that reside hidden within all, underneath the lies which so vociferously claim they are dead and so might as well be forgotten. That they have been forgotten in our lives is evident; that they must be remembered demonstrated by our alienation from one another and its resultant sorrow and pain. The opening lines of a poem by Christina Rossetti can be seen as a metaphor for what seems to have happened to harden our hearts, leaving us isolated in our separate interests, too often uncaring, cold, and as hard as ice.

> In the bleak midwinter,
> Frosty wind made moan,
> Earth stood hard as iron,
> Water like a stone;
> Snow had fallen, snow on snow,
> Snow on snow,
> In that bleak midwinter,
> Long ago.[66]

If we are to find our way out of the frozen past and back to the warmth of the present, that hardness of heart must be softened by the power of compassion. This means we must cease reinforcing its opposite through blame, comparison, and judgment. Being considerate, like becoming the master of one's fate, is an attitude to be cultivated by undoing—or unlearning—all it is not. Then blossoms the natural and the positive.

Since learning about becoming stronger is possible for everyone, at all times and in all places, let me give you another example of how, when we pay attention, we can learn something valuable about the right attitude from even the smallest things. In the 1972 movie *Jeremiah Johnson*, Jeremiah, played by Robert Redford, is a man fed up with city life in the 1850s who, with no experience, decides to go off by himself and live in the mountains.

There he comes upon an old grizzly hunter who befriends him and teaches him "mountain ways." After becoming proficient in this new way of life, Jeremiah meets and marries an Indian woman, adopts a traumatized orphan, and then builds a happy home life with both of them. Later, against his wishes, he leads a party of soldiers through a sacred Indian burial ground to rescue a wagon train stranded in the snow. He then rushes home only to find his wife and son murdered in repayment for his trespass, after which he sets out on a trail of vengeance.

He catches up with four of the murderers, kills three while being wounded himself, and then, feeling remorseful, lets the fourth one go. After his retaliation, the tribe sends forth one warrior after another after another to slay him. Jeremiah defeats them all. Finally, after he has become a great warrior in the eyes of the tribespeople, the chief arrives and gives Jeremiah the sign of peace, which means the war against him is over, and turns away.

At the story's conclusion, Jeremiah is high in the snow roasting a rabbit over a fire, when the old grizzly hunter comes upon him. The two of them greet each other and chat for a while. The old mountain man, who knows the legend Jeremiah has become, then sits down to eat with him, and they have this laconic dialogue:

> Mountain man: You've come far, pilgrim.
> Pause.
> Jeremiah: Feels like far.
> Mountain man: Were it worth the trouble?
> Pause.
> Jeremiah: Ah, what trouble?

That is *exactly* the attitude we should seek in regard to both our past difficulties and current problems. "Ah, what trouble?" is the outward expression of scorn toward what should be scorned: the weak-minded thinking that cries, "Why, oh why, is it always poor me?"

18

What Trumps All

Real Heroes

Now while Jeremiah Johnson is a movie, and the tale of the wise man who said "I see" is a fable, and the lama's aphorism is fictional, there are real-life stories of those who have more or less said the same to adversity. Admiral Stockdale responded to his terrible ordeal with, "So what?" Victor Frankl found his power to choose his attitude unweakened, even in the midst of a concentration camp. Socrates refused all offers to compromise or escape and faced his unjust execution with his usual composed attitude of "if it so be, so be it."[67]

These are the ones who should be listened to—the wise people of the world, whose universal themes are nearly unanimous: That the world is irrational. That it is necessary to put aside our shuffling about of things on the surface, which is like rearranging shadows. That there is a significant problem, that we are the source of that problem, and that it is up to us to work on its resolution, at least as it relates to ourselves.

And these, our real heroes, say what they say not because they care for personal posterity, but because they care for humankind—in other words, for us. However, while it is clear that the wise care *for* us, it is also clear they have not offered to take care *of* us. That's because they see us as alike to them. This is why the wise do not talk down to us or demean us. Instead, they constantly reinforce the idea that we are all worthy, telling us not only that we *can* make it to their state of mind, but also that we *will.*

The wise speak about all of us in different, interesting ways. Some liken us to diamonds in the rough, in need only of shedding the dross we still cling to and then following up with diligent self-polishing. Some say that when we finally face our inner darkness without flinching, we will discover that we are our own light. Still others tell us we are reasoning beings, simply lost and asleep in the dimly lit cave of ignorance, but slowly awakening to the awareness that there is a way out. But their basic messages are all the same. They all insist that our essential nature is the only reality, remaining undamaged, unmarked, and unmarred by error, no matter the size or number of our mistakes. They equally insist, however, that we will be capable of accepting this truth for ourselves only when we become willing to recognize it as being just as true for others.

The wise are united on this point as well: that mankind is caught in the terrifying confusion of the web of selfishness, saying that once we see this clearly, we will instantly recognize this: that it is the responsibility—and the privilege—of the less caught to be of assistance to the more caught; not so much by words or even actions, as by example.

According to them, what seems to separate us from our singularly satisfying purpose of being of comfort to others—and thereby ourselves—is an illusion of benefit laid out on a sharp-cornered table by self-centeredness and greed. In the Arthurian fable, King Arthur's table was round because all of the knights were seen to be of equal value. If we are to find true happiness, the wise declare, welcome and respect are what we must learn to offer others, even when their actions show they remain too afraid to come to their rightful places at the table. Those who have arrived, they say, live quietly in the absence of all doubt that others will find their way there too.

What about the rest of us? Where do you and I stand in proximity to that same round table? The answer to that question depends on where we stand in our own self-development. And this, in turn, depends on how close we have come to remembering that—ultimately—it is our conscience alone we each live with.

The Roman statesman and philosopher Cicero, ca. 50 BCE, suggested taking this little test to help us determine the state of our minds and the depth of our commitment to advancing to a more respectable state:

> Imagine yourself able to do something questionable that would bring to you excessive wealth, or power, or tyranny, or sensual satisfaction. Imagine further that no one were going to discover, or even suspect, what you were up to: on the contrary, that neither gods nor men would ever have an inkling about what you had done. Would you do it? Well, would you?[68]

For those who have learned the lesson that they must live with themselves, shadowy undertakings have lost all attraction. Therefore, to them, the only rational answer to Cicero's question is no.

And so at the end, the reality is that for our confusion to cease and our self-improvement to reach its potential, we must replace the amnesia of selfishness with the recognition of self-worth. Concomitant with this, the natural question that arises is: If we haven't embarked on our journey yet, then when? Remember that while the wise tell us that making it to where they are is *not* up to us, because that is guaranteed and therefore indisputable, they also say that *when* we will set out to do so is.

The final question is how to begin? The proper answer is simply this: with the first—and the last—step clearly in mind; the realization that because only kindness is unconditional and, therefore, unlimited, when all is said and done, *kindness trumps all.*

Acknowledgments

This book is for David, whose request for information about business and success was the motivation for my writing it. It is also for my children and my grandchildren, in fond hopes they may find value in some of its lessons.

It arrives with my thanks for the invaluable contribution of my editor Alison Owings, and to Chris Zook and Lynn Everett, who helped enormously in putting the finishing touches on it. Most of all my gratitude goes to Kenneth and Gloria Wapnick, for all they have taught me and all that they do, and of course, forever, to my beloved wife Kathy for her great friendship and constant help.

Endnotes

[1]   Christopher Byron, *Testosterone Inc.*, pp. 112–115.

[2]   Ibid., pp. 203–205, 217.

[3]   Voltaire from *Questions sur l'Encyclopédie*, "Droit," part 4, section I, 1771. "Il est défendu de tuer; tout meurtrier est puni, à moins qu'il n'ait tué en grande compagnie, et au son des trompettes." From *Oeuvres Complètes de Voltaire: Dictionnaire Philosophique,* http://www.voltaire-integral. com/Html/18/droit.htm.

[4]   Thomas Jefferson, Letter to John Wayes Eppes, June 24, 1813. Published in *The Writings of Thomas Jefferson,* vol. IX, p. 389.

[5]   Wendell Rawls Jr., *Cold Storage,* p. 186.

[6]   Lewis Carroll, *Alice's Adventures in Wonderland,* p. 54.

[7]   Peter C. Whybrow, M.D., *American Mania—When More Is Not Enough*, pp. 259–261.

[8]   Sigmund Freud, *Introductory Lectures on Psychoanalysis*, p. 493.

[9]   Philip Caputo, *A Rumor of War,* pp. 228–231.

[10]   Lauren R. Rubin, "Clear Skies, Plenty of Sun," *Barron's,* p. 28.

[11]   Johnny Miller, *I Call the Shots,* p. 40.

[12]   William Shakespeare, *Hamlet,* p. 132.

[13]   J. Krishnamurti, *The First and Last Freedom,* p. 185.

[14]   Kenneth Wapnick, *Love Does Not Oppose,* audio tape of workshop, April 1987. For more information on the Foundation for *A Course in Miracles,* visit www.facim.org.

[15]   Webster's Ninth New Collegiate Dictionary, 1988.

[16]   Fyodor Dostoevsky, *The Brothers Karamazov,* p. 313.

[17]   Whybrow, pp. 258, 259.

[18]   Cited in Walter Isaacson, *Einstein: His Life and Universe,* p. 273.

[19]   Epictetus, *The Discourses of Epictetus,* p. 12.

[20]   Plato, *Laws,* VIII, 831D, p. 1397.

[21]   Richard Feynman, *The Pleasure of Finding Things Out,* p. 108.

[22]   Walt Whitman, from the Preface of the 1855 edition of *The Leaves of Grass,* cited in Gay Wilson Allen, et. al., *Literary Criticism: Pope to Croce,* p. 401.

[23]   Epictetus, p. 107.

[24]   *I Ching,* p. 182.

[25]   Matthew Arnold, *Selected Poems,* p. 152, l. 60–66.

[26]   Henry David Thoreau, *Walden and Other Writings,* p. 111.

[27]   *The Bhagavad Gita,* p. 63.

[28]   Cited in Richard Alan Krieger, *Civilization's Quotations: Life's Ideal*, p. 178.

[29]   Wapnick, *Love Does Not Oppose.*

[30]   Epictetus, p. 135.

[31]   Spinoza, *Ethics and Selected Letters,* p. 153.

[32]   Plato, p. 197.

[33]   Aldous Huxley, *The Perennial Philosophy*, p. 103.

[34]   Sam and Chuck Giancana, *Double Cross,* pp. 255–256.

[35]   Epictetus, p. 13.

[36]   Stewart Emery, *Actualizations,* pp. 7–8.

[37]   Plato, p. 812.

[38]   Cited in Thomas Hornbein, *Everest—The West Ridge,* p. 171.

[39]   Kathy Galloway, *The Dream of Learning Our True Name,* p. 13.

[40]   Victor Frankl, *Man's Search for Meaning,* p. 65.

[41]   Webster's Ninth New Collegiate Dictionary.

[42]   Byron "Cowboy" Wolford, *Cowboys, Gamblers & Hustlers,* p. 139.

[43]   Ibid., p. 145.

[44]   Ibid., pp. 152–154.

[45]   Edward Conlon, *Blue Blood,* p. 170.

[46]   Plato, p. 349.

[47]   Webster's Ninth New Collegiate Dictionary.

[48]   Steve Forbes, "Golden Times—Even If We Don't Know It," *Forbes Magazine,* p. 27.

[49]   Tom Wolfe, "The Pirate Rose," *Conde Nast Portfolio,* p. 270.

[50]   Wapnick, *Sickness and Healing,* audio tape of workshop, July 1989.

[51]   Albert Camus, *The Myth of Sisyphus,* p. 121.

[52]   Theodor Reik, *Listening with the Third Ear,* pp. 141–142.

[53]   Montaigne, from the essay "Of Experience," *The Complete Essays of Montaigne,* pp. 850–851.

[54]   Originally published by Anne Herbert in 1977 and reprinted in Glen O. Gabbard, *Medical Marriages,* pp. 157–158.

[55]   Plato, p. 747.

[56]   James Bond Stockdale, *Courage Under Fire,* p. 9.

[57]   Ibid., p. 21.

[58]   Epictetus, p. 30.

[59]   Cormac McCarthy, *All the Pretty Horses,* p. 235.

[60]   Joyce Wethered, "Competitive Golf," *The American Golfer,* 1931. Reprinted in *Newsletter from the Society of Hickory Golfers,* March/April 2007, http://www.hickorygolfers. com/newslettertemplate.php?fn=mar07.php.

[61]   Cited in Isaacson, p. 333.

[62]   Friedrich Nietzsche, *Thus Spoke Zarathustra,* p. 24.

[63]   Dwight D. Eisenhower, "Chance for Peace," Speech before the American Society of Newspaper Editors, April 16, 1953. (www.eisenhowermemorial.org/speeches)

[64]   Matthew Arnold, p. 103. A longer excerpt from Arnold's poem "Dover Beach," from which this line is derived, is found after the title page of this book.

[65]   Epictetus, p. 9.

[66]   "In the Bleak Midwinter" was originally written by Christina Rossetti in 1872. The poem's words were later

set to music by Gustav Holst in 1906 and became a popular hymnal [www.cyberhymnal.org].

[67]   Plato, from the *Republic,* p. 577.

[68]   Cicero, *Select Orations,* p. 150.

Bibliography

Allen, Gay Wilson, Allan H. Gilbert, Harry Hayden Clark. *Literary Criticism: Pope to Croce.* Detroit, Michigan: Wayne State University Press, 1962.

Arnold, Matthew. *Selected Poems.* New York, New York: Penguin Books, 1994.

Bhagavad Gita. Translated by Barbara Stoler Miller. New York, New York: Columbia University Press, 1986.

Byron, Christopher. *Testosterone Inc.—Tales of CEOs Gone Wild.* Hoboken, New Jersey: John Wiley & Sons, 2004.

Camus, Albert. *The Myth of Sisyphus.* New York, New York: Vintage International, division of Random House, 1983.

Caputo, Philip. *A Rumor of War.* New York, New York: Holt, Reinhart and Winston, 1977.

Carroll, Lewis. *Alice's Adventures in Wonderland* and *Through the Looking Glass*. New York, New York: The Modern Library, 2002.

Cicero, Marcus Tullius. *Select Orations of Marcus Tullius Cicero*. Translated by C.D. Yonge. Eastchester, New York: The Translation Publishing Company, 1962.

Conlon, Edward. *Blue Blood*. New York, New York: Riverhead Books, 2004.

Dostoevsky, Fyodor. *The Brothers Karamazov*. New York, New York: Farrar Straus Giroux, 1990.

Emery, Stewart. *Actualizations: You Don't Have to Rehearse to Be Yourself*. New York, New York: Doubleday & Company, Inc., Dolphin Books, 1978.

Epictetus. *The Discourses of Epictetus*. Mount Vernon, New York: Peter Pauper Press, 1948.

Feynman, Richard. *The Pleasure of Finding Things Out*. Cambridge, Massachusetts: Perseus Books, 1999.

Forbes, Steve. 2007. "Golden Times—Even If We Don't Know It," *Forbes Magazine* (May 7): 27.

Frankl, Victor. *Man's Search for Meaning*. Boston, Massachusetts: Beacon Press, 2006.

Freud, Sigmund. *Introductory Lectures on Psychoanalysis*. New York, New York: Live Right, Division of W.W. Norton & Co., 1977.

Gabbard, Glen O. and Menninger, Roy W. *Medical Marriages*. Arlington, Virginia: American Psychiatric Publishing, 1988.

Galloway, Kathy. *The Dream of Learning Our True Name*. Glasgow, Scotland: Wild Goose Publications, 2004.

Giancana, Sam and Chuck. *Double Cross*. New York, New York: Warner Books, 1992.

Hornbein, Thomas. *Everest—The West Ridge*. San Francisco, California: Sierra Club, 1965.

Huxley, Aldous. *The Perennial Philosophy*. New York, New York: First Perennial Classics, imprint of HarperCollins, 2004.

I Ching. Translated by R. Whilhelm and C.F. Baynes. Princeton, New Jersey: Princeton University Press, Bollingen Series, 1990.

Isaacson, Walter. *Einstein: His Life and Universe*. New York, New York: Simon & Schuster, 2007.

Jefferson, Thomas. *The Writings of Thomas Jefferson*. Edited by Paul Leicester Ford. New York, New York: G.P. Putnam's Sons, 1883.

Krieger, Richard Alan. *Civilization's Quotations: Life's Ideal*. New York, New York: Algora Publishing, 2002.

Krishnamurti, J. *The First and Last Freedom*. San Francisco, California: HarperCollins, 1975.

McCarthy, Cormac. *All the Pretty Horses*. New York, New York: Vintage International, division of Random House, 1992.

Miller, Johnny. *I Call the Shots: Straight Talk About the Game of Golf Today*. New York, New York: Gotham Books, division of Penguin, 2004.

Montaigne. *The Complete Essays of Montaigne*. Translated by Donald M. Frame. Stanford, California: Stanford University Press, 1989.

Nietzsche, Friedrich. *Thus Spoke Zarathustra*. New York, New York: Penguin Classics, 2003.

Plato. *The Collected Dialogues of Plato*. Princeton, New Jersey: Princeton University Press, Bollingen Series, 1971.

Rawls, Wendell, Jr. *Cold Storage*. New York, New York: Simon & Schuster, 1980.

Reik, Theodor. *Listening with the Third Ear*. New York, New York: Farrar Straus Giroux, 1983.

Rubin, Lauren R. 2004. "Clear Skies, Plenty of Sun." *Barron's* (June 21): p. 28.

Shakespeare, William. *Hamlet*. Danbury, Connecticut: Harvard Classics, Grolier, 1980.

Spinoza, Baruch. *The Ethics and Selected Letters*. Translated by Samuel Shirley. Indianapolis, Indiana: Hackett Publishing Company, 1982.

Stockdale, James Bond. *Courage under Fire: Testing Epictetus's Doctrines in a Laboratory of Human Behavior*. Stanford, California: The Hoover Institution on War, Revolution and Peace, 1998.

Thoreau, Henry David. *Walden and Other Writings*. Edited by Joseph Wood Krutch. New York, New York: Bantam Books, 1982.

Voltaire, François-Marie Arouet. *Oeuvres Complètes de Voltaire: Dictionnaire Philosophique,* http://www.voltaire-integral.com/Html/00Table/4diction.htm

Wapnick, Kenneth. *Healing and Sickness.* Workshop audio tape (July 1989). Roscoe, New York: Foundation for *A Course in Miracles,* 1990.

Wapnick, Kenneth. *Love Does Not Oppose.* Workshop audio tape, Atlanta, Georgia (April 1987). Roscoe, New York: Foundation for *A Course in Miracles*, 1987.

Webster's Ninth New Collegiate Dictionary. Merriam Webster, Inc., 1988.

Wethered, Joyce. 1931. "Competitive Golf." *The American Golfer* 34 (1931).

Whybrow, Peter C., M.D. *American Mania—When More Is Not Enough.* New York, New York: W.W. Norton & Co., 2005.

Wolfe, Tom. 2007. "The Pirate Rose," *Conde Nast Portfolio* 1 (May 2007): 266–271.

Wolford, Byron "Cowboy." *Cowboys, Gamblers & Hustlers.* Las Vegas, Nevada: Cardsmith Publishing, 2002.

Printed in the United States
142655LV00005B/175/P

9 780595 527359